THE COLUMBIA RIVER SALMON AND STEELHEAD TROUT

BOOKS BY ANTHONY NETBOY

The Atlantic Salmon: A Vanishing Species?
The Salmon: Their Fight for Survival
Salmon: The World's Most Harassed Fish
Water, Land, and People (with Bernard Frank)

The

Columbia River Salmon

and

Steelhead Trout

Their Fight for Survival

ANTHONY NETBOY

UNIVERSITY OF WASHINGTON PRESS

Seattle and London

Library of Congress Cataloging in Publication Data

Netboy, Anthony.
    The Columbia River salmon and steelhead trout, their fight
for survival.

    Bibliography: p.
    Includes index.
    1. Salmon–fisheries—Columbia River—History.
2. Pacific salmon. 3. Steelhead (Fish)
4. Fishes—Effect of Dams on. 5. Fishes—
Columbia River. I. Title.
SH348.N39   333.95′6   80–50866
ISBN 0–295–95768–9

Dedicated to the biologists of the Oregon Fish and Wildlife Department, and all the other biologists as well as the sport and commercial fishermen who are striving to save what is left of the Columbia River salmon and steelhead trout against superhuman odds.

"If the salmon die, man is imperiled."—French proverb

Acknowledgments

I am greatly indebted to Leon Verhoeven, former director of the Pacific Marine Fisheries Commission, for his careful reading of the entire manuscript and his suggestions, to Robert Gunsolus of the Oregon Department of Fish and Wildlife for providing essential data, to Mrs. Gladys Seufert for permission to use material from the forthcoming memoirs of her husband, Francis Seufert, president of the Seufert Canning Company, and for her excellent photographs, and to Ed Chaney for the use of maps from his publication, *A Question of Balance.*

ANTHONY NETBOY

Jacksonville, Oregon
June, 1980

Contents

Illustrations

PHOTOGRAPHS (*following page 84*)

THE COLUMBIA RIVER SALMON AND STEELHEAD TROUT

CHAPTER 1

The Pristine River

The Columbia River rises in Columbia Lake, some 80 miles north of the United States border in British Columbia at an elevation of 2,650 feet above sea level. Starting as a rivulet on the silty formation called Canal Flats, which leads to Windermere Lake, a gemlike body of water nestling in the great trench between the Selkirks and the Rocky Mountains, the river emerges as a full-blown stream heading northwest through Kimbasket Lake toward the Arctic Ocean. After a course of about 200 miles it abruptly changes direction at a point near Boat Encampment called the Big Bend, and flows toward the Pacific Ocean. Leaving the trench, it turns southward, passes the Arrow Lakes, and enters the United States below Trail, in the northeast corner of the state of Washington, thus completing a journey of about 460 miles and dropping 1,360 feet in elevation. Between its confluence with the Okanogan near Brewster, Washington, and its meeting with the Snake River near Pasco and Kennewick, the Columbia forms another big bend, but counterclockwise this time, crossing the huge lava basin of the Columbia Plateau. Thence it soon forms the boundary between Oregon and Washington and heads for the Pacific in a westerly direction; at Portland, where it meets the Willamette River, it turns north-northwest toward Longview and then westerly until it reaches the sea at Astoria. At its mouth the river is five miles wide and forms a huge harbor, enabling ocean vessels to make their way to Portland. The total length of the Columbia is 1,270 miles, of which 745 miles are in the United States.

In its often tumultuous course, and especially after its confluence with the Snake, the Columbia in its pristine state was characterized by canyons and gorges, and flowed past timbered areas and benchlands. Between the mouth of the Okanogan and Priest Rapids there was a gorge with walls of black columnar basalt 1,000 to 3,000 feet high; below Rock Island, along the Cascade Mountains, and as the river passed through the Great Plain, there were spectacular foaming rapids and cascades like Celilo Falls, now alas wiped out by high dams.

In its lengthy course to the Pacific Ocean the Columbia flows through four mountain ranges, the Rockies, Selkirks, Cascades, and coastal mountains; in the east through arid stretches with scant rainfall and vegetation, and in the west through a region of abundant rainfall and luxuriant forests. The river drains 259,000 square miles, of which 39,500 square miles are in southeastern British Columbia, and pours more water into the ocean than any river in North America except the Saint Lawrence, Mississippi, and Mackenzie. It has a greater power potential than any other river system in the United States, and this has been a disaster, so to speak, for the salmonid resources, originally the richest in North America outside Alaska.

Hundreds of rivers pour their waters into the Columbia. The largest tributary, the Snake, is 1,038 miles long, issuing from Yellowstone National Park in Wyoming. Upon entering Idaho, the Snake sweeps in a westerly direction through the state, picking up tributaries, before turning northward to form the Idaho-Oregon border; at Lewiston it swings westerly again before entering Washington to join the Columbia near Pasco and Kennewick. The long middle section of the Snake crosses a plain of thick lava beds at an elevation of 3,000 to 5,000 feet. In this stretch most of the runoff comes from tributaries in the Sawtooth Mountains whose peaks rise to over 12,000 feet. The most spectacular section of the Snake is Hells Canyon, 33 miles long, on the Idaho-Oregon border, said to be the deepest gorge in North America if not the world, with sheer walls as high as 7,900 feet. Here the river is a wild, whirling stream. The Middle Snake accounts for a large portion of the Columbia's tremendous power potential.

In its pristine state the Columbia's flow fluctuated wildly. It was heaviest in late spring and early summer when the snow melted in the mountains, and in case of unusually warm and rainy spring weather the rain and snow cascaded down the slopes, filling rivers, creeks, and other watercourses; in late summer and early autumn, when the summits were almost bare, the flow was lightest. The full brunt of the torrent was perhaps best observed around Celilo

Falls. Here the river, breaking into several channels, flowed through a canyon 400 yards wide, broken by protruding rocks and promontories. Francis Seufert, last president of the Seufert Canning Company at The Dalles, Oregon, said that the river would rise 50 feet between low and high water: "The spring flood would start in April and generally crest the first week in June, then start to fall. At its crest the river was full of whirlpools, boils, and rushing water. A boat could not operate in it and a man who fell in was dead. Trees, logs, driftwood of all sizes came down and were tossed like corks. The river rose in the narrows to flood the rocks, came out of the channels and filled every crevice it could find with fast, rushing water. In September it was nearly as quiet and still as a lake."[1]

Periodically the Columbia went on a terrible rampage. One of those years was 1948. The main stem and some of the tributaries became scenes of devastation along hundreds of miles. Farms, factories, warehouses, mills, and homes were inundated or wrecked. Many lives were lost, many cattle were drowned. The entire city of Vanport, the second largest in Oregon, lying at the confluence of the Columbia and the Willamette, was completely wiped out, and much of downtown Portland was under water.

It is hard to picture the Columbia before the watershed was settled by white men, before cutting began in the lush evergreen forests where the Douglas fir reached 250 feet, clear of branches for over a hundred, and other evergreens nearly as high, the sod was broken for agriculture, cattle and sheep were stocked on the plains, and towns and cities arose. West of the Cascades, the landscape unfolded in an undulating panorama of trees with numerous streams meandering through the thickly carpeted forests. The air was sweet and clean, and the rivers, teeming with fish, ran pure and clear except after heavy rains. Indians traveled along the deer or elk trails on foot or horseback, or paddled their canoes on the swift streams. The brown semiarid region east of the Cascades, sparsely populated with aborigines, had its special beauty.

It is estimated that perhaps as many as 50,000 red men lived in the watershed area when Captains Lewis and Clark led their expedition through the Snake River area to the Columbia and the Pacific Ocean, in 1805–6. The aborigines had dwelled here for perhaps 10,000 years. Stone Age people—they were hunters and gatherers—did not turn the sod or plant seeds, were ignorant of the wheel and the plow, thus scarcely marred the biotic communities or disturbed much of the abundant and varied wildlife. Neither did they diminish the cornucopia of salmon, trout, sturgeon (weighing up to 1,500 pounds), smelt, and other fishes, some of which were the mainstay of their diet. They lived in harmony with nature; and their religion, based on the worship of animals and natural forces, gave them support for the adversities of human life.

When the Indians were lords of the land, myriad waterfowl came down to the rivers in the fall to feed, and returned in the spring to rest and feed before journeying to their northern winter breeding grounds. The rivers and numerous ponds, marshes, sloughs, and lakes were filled with ducks and geese, herons and cranes, sometimes with pelicans, and the estuaries with terns, plover, and other shore birds. Sea otters and seals, valued for their pelts, roamed in the bays and sometimes inshore. Golden and bald eagles, condors (largest birds in North America, now on the verge of extinction), ospreys, falcons, and hawks roosted in trees and on the promontories of the rocks. The melancholy calls of coyotes, foxes, and wolves filled the nights; bears sometimes came to the Indian villages to forage for food. Big game was plentiful in the forested and nonforested areas, as the *Journals* of Captains Lewis and Clark reveal. They saw many deer and elk (and ate their meat), antelope, mountain lion, bobcat or lynx, fisher, marten, and beaver; hare, rabbits, and squirrels were in abundance, as well as polecat or skunk. The woods were rich in berries, acorns, and other nuts, and bulbs delicious to the aborigines.

We can obtain glimpses of the Columbia from the diaries of early explorers. The young Scottish plant hunter David Douglas, for whom the region's most valuable timber tree is named, though he did not discover it, made three journeys in the valley in the years 1825–27. He was enraptured with the scenery along the river and its environs, particularly by the towering snow-clad peaks, such as Hood, Adams, and Saint Helens.

So rich was the region with wildflowers and plants that Douglas collected and sent back to England seeds and dried specimens of hundreds of species unknown in Europe including grape, wild hyacinth, dogwood, various fir, pines, especially the sugar pine, mountain pink, California poppy, Mariposa lily, mimulus, twenty-one species of lupine, eleven species of primrose, numerous berries, currants, and native tobacco.

Here is the scene near Cape Shoalwater at the entrance to Willapa Bay, where Douglas and his Indian guides pitched their tent, after a long day botanizing, near a stream, their clothes soaked by continuous rain. "A little before dusk," he says in his diary, "the weather moderated, when I crawled out with my gun; I killed five ducks with one shot, which, as might be expected, were soon cooked; one of the Indians ate a part raw, the other did not take time to pluck the feathers but literally burned them to save time. . . . I made a basin of tea, on which, with a bit of duck, I made a good supper. Very little sufficed me."[2]

He was enchanted with the Grand Rapids at a time when the river was low: "The scenery . . . is likewise grand beyond description; the high mountains in the neighbourhood, which are for the most part covered with pines of several species, some of which grow to an enormous size, are all loaded with snow; the rainbow from the vapour of the agitated water, which rushes with furious rapidity over shattered rocks and through deep canyons producing an agreeable although at the same time a somewhat melancholy echo through the thick wooded valley; the reflections from the snow on the mountain, together with the vivid green of the gigantic pines, form a contrast of rural grandeur that can scarcely be surpassed."[3]

John Kirk Townsend was a naturalist who in 1832 crossed the continent with the Boston merchant Nathaniel Wyeth, who planned to organize a trade in fish and furs. In his memoirs Townsend describes many scenes on the "noble Columbia": "About noon we struck the Walla-Walla river, a very pretty stream of fifty or sixty yards in width, fringed with tall willows, and containing a number of salmon, which we can see frequently leaping from the water. The pasture here, being good, we allowed our horses an hour's rest to feed, and then travelled on over the plain, until near dark, when, on rising a sandy hill, the noble Columbia burst at once upon our view. I could scarcely repress a loud exclamation of delight and pleasure, as I gazed upon the magnificent river, flowing silently and majestically on, and reflected that I had actually crossed the vast American continent, and now stood upon a stream that poured its waters directly into the Pacific."[4]

In this area of little rain, Townsend says, "the banks are in many places high and rocky, occasionally interrupted by broad, level sandy beaches. The only vegetation along the margin, is the wormwood, and other low, arid plants, but some of the bottoms are covered with heavy, rank grass, affording excellent pasture for horses" (p. 282). As his party traveled along the Walla Walla they

were visited by Indians "whose wigwams we see on the opposite
side of the river. As we approach these rude huts, the inhabitants
. . . come forth in a body; a canoe is immediately launched, the
light bark skims the water like a bird, and in an incredibly short
time its inmates are with us. Sometimes a few salmon are brought
to barter for our tobacco, paint, etc." (p. 283).

The Indians who lived along the Columbia and Snake rivers
were divided into numerous tribes, from the Shoshones and Nez
Perce in Idaho to the Chinook, Clatsop, Cathlamet, Clackamas,
Clatskanie, and Wishram in the tidewater area, usually in villages
of up to a score of houses. They lived off the land, were skilled
in fishing and hunting with the bow and arrow, and in basketry
and woodcraft, especially in making canoes, some of which were
40 feet long. They wore little clothing, particularly in the warmer
areas, went barefoot, or tramped in deerskin moccasins through
the wet forests. Many of the tribes had horses, and most of them
had dogs used for food as well as pets. Cultural levels were varied.
None had a written language, dialects were numerous, and eastern
tribes could not communicate with the western until a kind of
lingua franca was invented by the mercantile Chinook, who were
great traders, after the white men came into their world.

The salmon and other fish in the rivers, abundant game in the
woods, numerous waterfowl, and roots and berries almost everywhere provided an ample food supply, easily obtained. As Captain
Clark, who with Captain Lewis came to know the Indians well,
wrote in his diary at one point, "This village lay in the prosperous
area of the jumping salmon where life was good and where the red
men had time to contemplate nature and God."

One must not, however, imagine that the "noble savages" led
the kind of idyllic lives depicted in the writings of Rousseau,
Chateaubriand, and James Fenimore Cooper. They were subjected
to diseases with which they could not cope, for they had no
medicines or antidotes, especially after the white men introduced
some of their infections. Lewis and Clark commented frequently
in their journals on the prevalence of sickness among the Indians,
especially their bad eyes and lack of hygiene. In brief, although
there were many old people among them, if we take the Lewis and
Clark diaries as reporting typical populations, their existence, on
the whole, was "short and brutish."

When Captain Robert Gray on May 11, 1792, sailed his vessel,
the 212-ton *Columbia Rediviva,* across a treacherous bar and discov-

ered the river which he named after his ship, and which explorers like Captain Cook and Admiral Vancouver had missed, he introduced a new era in the life of the aborigines. Unwittingly, he set in motion changes that were to shatter their world, profoundly alter the mighty river and much of its watershed within a century and a half, and lead to severe diminution of wildlife and fisheries, especially the salmon. It is a story not well known but needing to be told, particularly at this time when the fish runs are severely diminished and the Columbia is, in fact, from the end of tidewater to its headwaters, no longer a river but a chain of reservoirs, except for a 50-mile stretch of free-flowing water in the Hanford Reservation area.

CHAPTER 2

The Indian Fisheries

The plethora of salmon and steelhead trout and other fishes and the manner in which the Indians harvested them astonished the early explorers. There is evidence that it was the abundance of fish and drinking water that attracted the aborigines who came to the North Pacific Coast from Asia at a time when a land bridge connected the two continents. The cycle of salmon and other anadromous fish appearing and disappearing from the rivers ruled the rhythm of Indian life, for without a fish supply they were in danger of starving, as Lewis and Clark noted. Some of the tribes had summer and winter homes: the wooden houses were dismantled at the end of winter and the timbers were stored and reassembled when the occupants returned from their spring and summer fishing, hunting, and trading activities. Other tribes were more or less stationary. Fishing was concentrated at natural barriers, especially waterfalls which held up the migratory fish and allowed them to be caught easily, as at Kettle Falls in northern Washington, Celilo Falls on the lower Columbia River (drowned by The Dalles Dam), and at various key places on the tributaries, such as along the Sanpoil, Okanogan, Spokane Falls, Yakima, Grande Ronde, Umatilla, Deschutes, Klickitat, and Willamette Falls. Salmon were also caught in bays and sloughs, with spears, harpoons, dipnets, hook and line, and on a larger scale with seines, traps, and weirs—virtually all the devices later used by the white men.

Men did the fishing and hunting and women the preparation and curing of the fish and meat. Salmon and meat were broiled, either by being wedged on a split stick or impaled and held over a fire. Hot stones placed in a basket were used for boiling fish.

Sometimes an elk hide sunk in a pit served as a vessel. Steam cooking was also known to the Indians, and fish were smoked or dried and pulverized by rubbing between stones, producing a product called pemmican, which could be stored for a long time.

Some of the gear employed by the Indians was comparable in quality and efficiency to the white man's before the development of nylon netting and other modern materials. Nets were up to 8 feet deep and 300 feet long; one end was kept on shore, held fast with wooden stakes, and the other was taken out in a canoe and circled around the area where the fish were believed to pass, usually close to the riverbank. When the fish were in the net, both ends were pulled in, care being taken to keep the rock "lead line" on the bottom and slightly ahead of the wooden "cork line." As the operation was completed the salmon were trapped in the constricting net and hauled onto the beach. This kind of fishing required teamwork, for which the Indians were well organized.

Sometimes the Indians fished from canoes, using bone hooks and lines to which smelt were attached as bait; a stone sinker kept the line steady. They also used a gig (that is, a spear) to take salmon, sturgeon, and other large fish. A common method of communal fishing was the erection of a weir, consisting of brush and saplings supported by willow stakes to which baskets were attached. Once caught in the mesh, the fish could not turn around and were taken out by untying the hull of the basket. Weirs were most successful in narrow channels, and were taken down when a sufficient supply of fish had been caught. Lewis and Clark drew accurate sketches of these contraptions observed in the Columbia River. Among some tribes in the Pacific Northwest, as on the Klamath River, the erection of a weir was accompanied by minute and strict religious rites and taboos.

"Usual and Accustomed Fishing Places"

The earliest report on the salmon's abundance and the Indian fishery was published in 1814 in Nicholas Biddle's *History of the Expedition under the Command of Captains Lewis and Clark.* It reveals the remarkable knowledge the aborigines had of the salmon in the Columbia River and how they exploited them. The runs were continuous from April to November, although fluctuating at times. Chinook came in spring, summer, and fall runs; sockeye (blueback) ran from May to early September; silvers (coho) came in summer and ran till the leaves turned color in the deciduous trees. There were also chum or dog salmon, and seagoing trout. Many glimpses of the role salmon played in aboriginal life are found in the *Journals* of Lewis and Clark. On October 17, 1805, Clark noted at a place probably on the Yakima River:

> I took *two* men in a Small canoe and assended the Columbia river 10 miles to an Island near the Stard. Shore [starboard shore] on which two large Mat Lodges of Indians were drying Salmon, The number of dead Salmon on the Shores & floating in the river is incrediable to say—and at this Season they have only to collect the fish Split them open and dry them on their Scaffolds on which they have great numbers, how far they have to raft their timber they make their scaffolds of I could not lern; but there is no timber of any sort except Small willow bushes in sight in any direction. from this Island the natives showed me the enterance of a large Westerly fork . . . about 8 miles distant, the evening being late I deturmined to return to the forks, at which place I reached at Dark. passed a Island in the middle of the river at 5 miles at the head of which is a rapid, not dangerous[.] on the Lard. Side [starboard side] opposit to this rapid is a fishing place 3 Mat Lodges, and great quants. of Salmon on scaffolds drying. Saw great numbers of Dead Salmon on the Shores and floating in the water, great numbers of Indians on the banks viewing me and 18 canoes accompanied me from the point. The waters of this river is clear, and a Salmon may be seen at the deabth of 15 or 20 feet. . . . passed three large lodges on the Star. Side near which great number of Salmon was drying on scaffolds[.] one of those Mat lodges I entered[.] found it crouded with men women and children and near the enterance of those houses I saw maney squars engaged [in] splitting and drying Salmon. I was furnished with a mat to set on, and one man set about preparing me something to eate, first he brought in a piece of a Drift log of pine and with a wedge of the elks horn, and a malet of Stone curioesly carved he Split the log into Small pieces and lay'd it open on the fire on which he put round Stones, a woman handed him a basket of water and a large Salmon about half Dried, when the Stones were hot he put them into the basket of water with the fish which was soon sufficiently boiled for use[.] it was then taken out put on a platter of rushes neetly made, and set before me[.] they boiled a Salmon for each of the men with me, dureing those preparations, I smoked, with those about me who chose to smoke which was but fiew, this being a custom those people are but little accustomed to and only Smok thro: form. after eateing the boiled fish which was delicious, I set out & halted or come too on the Island at the two Lodges, Several fish was given to me, in return for Which I gave Small pieces of ribbond.[1]

At Celilo Falls David Douglas saw Indians hauling out scores of salmon from foaming white waters. "He spent hours," says his biographer William Morwood, "observing the various netting and trapping techniques employed. The more daring tribesmen worked from planks suspended over the water. They dipped with long poles equipped with nets and periodically came up with a struggling salmon." Douglas wrote in his diary, "The fish are of good quality, much about the same size (15 to 25 lbs.) as those caught in the rivers of Europe." Later, on the Spokane River, he estimated the daily catch at about two thousand salmon.[2]

In his memoirs, Alexander Ross, a member of the North West Company, later incorporated into the Hudson's Bay Company, described Indian fishing on the Okanogan River in 1825. These people passed their summers securing part of their annual food supply, mainly fish, roots, and berries. In the middle of June "they all assemble again in large bands on the banks of the different rivers. [Weirs are constructed] by the united labour of the whole village or camp assembled in one place. The salmon being in the utmost abundance . . . , one or more of the principal men are appointed, by general consent, to superintend each. The person or persons thus chosen divide the fish every morning. . . . Their authority is law in all those matters till the end of the fishing season, which is generally about the beginning of October. . . . The fish, when properly cured, is packed up into large bundles or bales; the roots and berries into bags made of rushes." During the night these packages were cached in secret places, "each family having its share apart, secure from wild beasts and the eye of thieves." During the fishing season life was not all hard work: "Gambling, dancing, horseracing, and frolicking, in all its varied forms, are continued without intermission; and few there are, even the most dull and phlegmatic, who do not feel, after enjoying so much hilarity, a deep regret on leaving the piscatory camp." After the fishing season the natives withdrew into the mountainous interior for the purpose of snaring deer, elk, and other game, and after a month or more in this pursuit they settled down for the winter in their permanent habitations on the banks of small streams.[3]

Lewis and Clark saw Indians fishing at over a hundred stations on the Columbia below the Wenatchee River. In one day they passed twenty-nine lodges where they were catching and drying fish. Outside nearly every hut hung stacks of drying fish. On October 22, 1805, Captain Clark observed, in the vicinity of Celilo Falls, Indians preparing pemmican: "After [being] suffi[ci]ently Dried [the fish] is pounded between Two Stones fine, and put into a speces of basket neetly made of grass and rushes better than two feet long and one foot Diamiter . . . lined with the Skin of Salmon Stretched and dried for the purpose, in this it is pressed down as hard as is possible, when full they Secure the open part with the fish Skins across which they fasten th[r]o. the loops of the basket that part very securely, and then on a Dry Situation they Set those baskets the corded part up, their common custome is to Set 7 as close as they can Stand and 5 on the top of them, . . . those 12 baskets of from 90 to 100 lbs. each form a Stack. thus preserved those fish may be kept Sound and sweet Several years, as those people inform me, Great quantities . . . are sold to the whites people who visit the mouth of this river as well as to the nativs below."[4] At one village Clark counted 107 stacks totaling at least 10,000 pounds.

Craig and Hacker in their classic study, *The History and Development of the Fisheries of the Columbia River,* estimate that if the population of the Columbia River watershed was 50,000 persons and every man, woman, and child consumed about a pound of salmon a day, the annual catch was around 18 million pounds, or two to three times total landings annually from the Columbia River in recent years (excluding ocean catches).

The Celilo Fishery

To visualize the aboriginal fishery in its most spectacular form we must betake ourselves to Celilo Falls, the Long Narrows of the Columbia. Here the pellucid river after a journey of about 1,000 miles dropped into a long, narrow, deep chasm, broken by small islands and protruding rocks and falls, all of which provided ideal if treacherous fishing spots. The Oregon side was controlled by the Wasco band of the Chinook tribe, the Washington side by the Wishrams. The Wyams also held sway on the south bank. Here came Indians from the interior who had no fishing grounds of their own or whose fishing was poor, to trade for dried salmon, offering peltries from Montana, jade axes from the Fraser River area, horn of mountain sheep, baskets, rabbit, or bearskin robes. The Klamath and Modoc peoples from Klamath Lake brought slaves and dentalia shells, their medium of exchange. "Trade connections with the The Dalles," says the anthropologist Philip Drucker, in *Cultures of the North Pacific Coast,* "stretched across the Rockies and into the Great Plains."

Standing on slippery rocks or precarious wooden platforms,

really scaffolding, with the river churning and boiling below, the roped fishermen caught the salmon with nets, or speared them as they leaped up from the water in a desperate attempt to climb the falls or negotiate them somehow to reach their spawning grounds; if they fell back, they made another attempt, again and again. Sometimes the fisherman was lowered in a basket down the sheer side of the rock; here he waited until a large fish came up, which he speared and put into his net, and was then lifted by his companion to the platform. A man had to be alert and agile to land a chinook weighing 50 pounds or more with a dipnet from a narrow perch. If he fell into the cold waters, he was dead in a few minutes. All fishing then stopped for the day.

Fishing stands on the rocks and islands were a family inheritance, passed down from father to sons. Through marriage, inheritance, payment for wives, and occasional purchases, ownerships became scattered and an individual might have a share in a productive eddy or pool far from his native village.

Fishing began at dawn and ended at dusk. One person caught all his family could clean in a day and then another took his place. Ten or twelve persons might fish from one stand in the course of the day. Strangers might be given an opportunity to fish if their needs were great, for this was a subsistence fishery with the surplus used for barter. The Chinook were called "mercantile Indians" because they had a strongly developed sense of trade.

There was an impressive ancient fishery at the falls of the Willamette River, visited by Lieutenant Charles Wilkes, in charge of a Pacific expedition in 1838–42. He described the "novel as well as amusing scene":

> The salmon leap the fall; and it would be inconceivable, if not actually witnessed, how they can force themselves up, and after a leap of from ten to twelve feet retain strength enough to stem the force of the water above. About one in ten of those who jumped, would succeed in getting by. They are seen to dart out of the foam beneath and reach about two-thirds of the height, at a single bound: those that thus passed the apex of the running water, succeed; but all that fell short, were thrown back again into the foam. I never saw so many fish collected together before; and the Indians are constantly employed in taking them. They rig out two stout poles, long enough to project over the foaming cauldron, and secure their larger ends to the rocks. On the outer end they make a platform for the fisherman to stand on, . . . perched on it with a pole thirty feet long in hand, to which the net is fastened by a hoop four feet in diameter. . . . The mode of using the net is peculiar: they throw it in the foam as far up

the stream as they can reach, and . . . the fish who are running up in a contrary direction are caught. Sometimes twenty large fish are taken by a single person in an hour; and it is only surprising that twice as many should not be caught.[5]

The natives also fished at the foot of the falls, where it was much safer. Wilkes estimated that about seventy men fished in this locality; counting those who fished from canoes, the number may have been a hundred. Most of them lived in nearby villages where there are now twin cities, Oregon City and West Linn, and a complex of pulp and paper mills. The Indians long ago disappeared from this area.

The Deified Salmon

The aborigines did not take their food animals for granted. They regarded them with awe and veneration. The fish thronged the streams and returned with astonishing punctuality every year to the rivers. After a brief rest, they moved upstream and headed for natal waters. After spawning all the salmon died, their lean and discolored bodies littering the banks of the rivers and ultimately disintegrating and drifting downstream. The next year the fish (actually another generation) reappeared.

"What was more logical," says Philip Drucker, "than the concept that the salmon ascended the streams to benefit mankind, died, and then returned to life?" Thus arose the belief "that the salmon were a race of supernatural beings who dwelt in a great house under the sea. There they went about in human form, feasting and dancing like people. When the time came for the 'run,' the salmon-people dressed in garments of salmon flesh, that is, assumed the form of fish to sacrifice themselves. Once dead, the spirit of each fish returned to the house beneath the sea. If the bones were returned to the water, the being resumed his form with no discomfort and could repeat the trip the next season."[6] It was evident that the fishes' migration was a purely voluntary act; therefore it behooved human beings to be extremely careful not to offend them, for they might refuse to return to the river, and that would be a calamity.

Nearly every tribe dependent on the salmon as the mainstay of their diet developed rituals and taboos to mark the arrival of the first fishes in the spring. The new arrivals were greeted with prayers and incantations to show the people's gratitude, joy, and relief, for if they did not appear, hunger would ensue. Captain Clark reports in his diary on April 19, 1806, when the expedition was on its way home, the arrival of the first salmon at a village below the Long Narrows: "There was great joy with the natives last night in consequence of the arrival of the Salmon; one of those fish was caught, this was the harbenger of good news to them. They informed us that those fish would arrive in great quantities in the course of about 5 days. this fish was dressed and being divided into small pieces was given to each child in the village. this custom is founded on a supersticious opinion that it will hasten the arrival of the Salmon."[7] Among some tribes the first-caught salmon was treated as if it were a visiting chief of high renown and accorded due honors.

On Sunday, April 20, 1956, when The Dalles Dam was about to be enclosed and the Celilo fishery, dating back to a long-forgotten time, would be inundated, I witnessed the last of the First Salmon rites held at Celilo village. The day was warm and sunny, and hundreds of tribesmen gathered for this sad occasion on the banks of the Columbia, the women wearing multicolored, flowing dresses and scarves, and the men awkward-fitting store clothes. Emissaries of Tommy Thompson, chief of the host band, the Wyams, said to be over a hundred years old, had to seek elsewhere than the Columbia for the salmon, because an early spring thaw in the mountains made it impossible to use the historic site to catch enough fish for the festival. They bought 400 pounds of salmon in Portland and members of the Warm Springs Reservation, who had fishing rights at Celilo, helped out with donations of venison and roots needed for the occasion.

The stolid, bronze-colored chief sat at the head table in the longhouse, surrounded by silent and respectful tribesmen squatting on mats on the earthen floor. Outside, slabs of salmon were being smoked over log fires tended by women, just as when Lewis and Clark camped here in 1805 and smoked a pipe of peace with the chiefs.

Chief Thompson blessed the first fish caught a few days before and made a speech in his native language that was charged with emotion. Before it was over the vigorous old man was weeping. Although I did not understand a word, I could imagine the feelings that inspired him as he saw the last bit of land held by the tribe about to go under water and the ancient picturesque fishery disappear. He had seen the white settlers pour into the valley, and the baleful impact they made on the natives' culture. The churning river where he had fished as a youth, from rickety platforms, would become a placid lake. There were tears in the eyes of many people who listened to him.

When the First Salmon rites were concluded the chief permitted newsmen to photograph him with his younger wife, Flora. Usually the festival lasted a few days, but this time it was confined to one day. There were bone games in the afternoon and dances in the evening. Next morning the Portland *Oregonian* reported an interview with Henry Thompson, son of the chief. "When the dam is finished," he said, "and there are no more fish at Celilo, my father will still live here, and will die here. I, too, will die here. Both of us were born at Celilo, and here," pointing to the Indian cemetery on a bluff above the village amid the rimrock, "we will be buried."

Tommy Thompson died three years later, and without him, without the roaring falls, and with salmon caught elsewhere, the First Salmon ceremonies held occasionally at the new Celilo village, built by the Corps of Engineers on the bluff, lost their flavor and meaning and were eventually abandoned.

CHAPTER 3

The Fisheries
in an Age of Abundance

Although the Oregon country was first explored and exploited by
white men searching for furs, principally beaver that could be sold
in Europe and China at a fabulous profit, the commercial possibilities of the rich salmon fisheries were not entirely overlooked. By
1823 the Hudson's Bay Company was packing salmon at Fort
George near Astoria. However, Fort Langley on the Fraser River
was regarded as a more suitable locality for this business, and here
a profitable saltery was established in 1827.

American traders endeavoring to exploit the fisheries at first met
with little success. In 1829 Captain John Dennis, commanding the
brig *Owyhee,* entered the Columbia River to pick up a cargo of
salmon, spent two summers in the area, and packed only fifty
barrels. He purchased the fish from the Indians, chiefly in exchange for tobacco, and delivered the cargo in Boston in a journey
around Cape Horn, where it sold for ten cents a pound.

Captain Nathaniel Wyeth made a fruitless overland trip to the
Columbia River in 1832, returned two years later on a combined
fur trading and salmon fishing venture, and established a trading
post on Sauvie Island at the mouth of the Willamette, long inhab-
ited by Indians. This venture too was a failure. Other easterners
were more successful. Captain John Couch of Newburyport, Mas-
sachusetts, one of the founders of Portland, reached the Columbia
in 1840, packed a cargo of fish, and returned home. He came back
two years later and established salteries at Willamette Falls and
Pillar Rock on the Columbia.

After the boundary dispute with England was settled in 1846,
Americans were able to make greater headway in the salmon trade
and the British faded out of the picture. By 1854 large quantities

19

of fish were being salted around Astoria and at the Cascades 150 miles upstream (now submerged by the Bonneville reservoir). Columbia River salmon was being shipped by water to the east coast, Hawaii (then known as the Sandwich Islands), and Chile. The delectable chinook was a familiar morsel in households of the Boston Brahmins, British aristocrats, and Latin American nabobs.

In the 1850s Hodgkins and Sanders began to fish for salmon with gillnets at Oak Point, 60 miles above Portland, while Jotham Reed was catching salmon in his fish traps at the same locality. Salteries were operating near the mouth of the river and at the Cascades. In 1863 Jotham Reed and H. N. Rice produced a thousand barrels of salted salmon and the next year two thousand barrels. Other firms entered the business, the market was soon oversupplied, and the price fell from twelve dollars to six dollars a barrel. Most of the product went to the Hawaiian Islands and a small part to the eastern states.

Enter the Canners

Canned foods, which revolutionized the diet of the lower classes, first appeared in France in the days of Napoleon Bonaparte, who needed to feed masses of troops on the march and while under gunfire. Canning was an ingenious method of preserving meat, fish, fruit, vegetables, even milk, in glass bottles, and later in tin canisters. It was convenient, cheap, and if properly handled, taking note, as Reay Tannahill says in *Food in History,* "of Louis Pasteur's discoveries about the part played by microorganisms in fermentation and putrefaction," was reliable as well. The first successful preservation of fish in tin canisters is attributed to Ezra Daggett, who was canning oysters and cod in New York City in 1819. In 1825 John Moir was canning salmon in Aberdeen, Scotland.

The first salmon cannery in North America was established by the brothers George W. and William Hume and Andrew S. Hapgood, all from Maine, on a raft in the Sacramento River in 1864. Two years later they moved to the Columbia, where they thought there was a more reliable supply of salmon, and erected a primitive cannery at a place they called Eagle Cliff on the Washington side. That year they produced 6,000 cases of 48 one-pound cans, all by hand.

The industry expanded rapidly. Canneries arose on both banks of the river, at Astoria, Ilwaco and Westport, Portland, The Dalles, and even on the Deschutes River. Nearly every major coastal stream in Oregon had one or more canneries. By 1874 there were twelve between Astoria and Portland, and by 1883 fifty-five on or near the Columbia, packing 630,000 cases of 48 one-pound cans valued at $3 million, using only chinook. In many areas on the Pacific coast, from the Sacramento to the Bering Sea, investors were rushing to tap this new "gold mine," including many foreigners; fortunes were made and lost as in other booming speculative industries. The Sacramento, Fraser, and prolific Alaska rivers were intensively fished as canned salmon became a popular and inexpensive food around the world. The chinook catch reached a peak of 43 million pounds on the Columbia in 1883, coincident with the operation of the maximum number of canneries. By 1890, when the chinook runs were manifestly declining and smaller species of salmon were being used for canning, which then took the bulk of the catches, the number of canneries had dropped sharply and the pack fell to an average of 385,000 cases annually in the years 1886–90 (tables 1 and 2).

At first Indians did the fishing for the packers, using mainly gillnets from small boats equipped with sails. They were augmented by Finns, Danes, Norwegians, and other foreigners as the industry expanded, usually fishing under contract with the packers. Astoria was the center of the industry, a Scandinavian town with Finnish and other Scandinavian names on the shops, and newspapers in foreign languages. Eventually some of the fishermen formed cooperatives in order to be free of company control. They adopted the policy that the entire catch of every member must be purchased by the cannery if it passed the quality test.

The canneries were sheds built on pilings at the river's edge. The fish were delivered directly to them, then were cleaned, slimed, and cut to fit a one-pound can that included the back and belly. The cans were filled, salted, placed in a retort and cooked under ten pounds of pressure for an hour, then cooled, washed, labeled, and boxed, all by hand. The basic procedure has not changed to this day, except that nearly all of the processes are automated, the number of hands greatly reduced, and the sanitation improved.

Most of the workers were nimble-fingered Chinese who

TABLE 1

AVERAGE ANNUAL COLUMBIA RIVER COMMERCIAL SALMON AND STEELHEAD
TROUT LANDINGS, EXCLUDING TROLL CATCHES, BY SPECIES, 1866–1963
(in million pounds)

Years	Chinook	Sockeye	Coho	Chum	Steelhead	Total
1866–70	4.1	. . .	. . .	. . .	. . .	4.1
1871–75	19.4	. . .	. . .	. . .	. . .	19.4
1876–80	31.3	. . .	. . .	. . .	. . .	31.3
1881–85	39.4	. . .	. . .	. . .	. . .	39.4
1886–90	24.2	1.0	. . .	. . .	0.9	26.1
1891–95	24.2	2.4	2.4	0.3	3.7	33.0
1896–1900	23.3	1.8	3.3	0.4	2.1	30.9
1901–05	28.9	0.8	1.4	1.1	0.6	32.8
1906–10	23.3	0.7	2.9	2.2	0.6	29.7
1911–15	27.0	0.9	3.5	3.0	1.9	36.3
1916–20	30.4	0.8	4.5	3.5	2.0	41.2
1921–25	22.0	1.2	6.2	2.1	2.4	33.9
1926–30	20.3	0.7	6.0	4.0	2.9	33.9
1931–35	18.2	0.3	3.4	1.1	1.8	24.8
1936–40	14.8	0.3	1.8	1.5	2.1	20.5
1941–45	16.1	0.2	1.2	2.2	1.9	21.6
1946–50	14.0	0.2	1.1	0.7	1.3	17.3
1951–55	7.7	0.3	0.7	0.3	1.5	10.5
1956–60	5.9	0.5	0.3	. . .	0.7	7.4
1961–63	4.7	0.1	0.5	. . .	0.8	6.1

SOURCE: A. T. Pruter, "Commercial Fisheries of the Columbia River and
Adjacent Ocean Waters," *Fishery Industrial Research* (Washington, D.C.: U.S.
Bureau of Commercial Fisheries), 3 (1966): 17-68.

NOTE: Troll catches are excluded because they contain an unknown
proportion of salmon from the Columbia River; that is, not all troll-caught
salmon landed in Columbia River district ports are of Columbia River
origin.

could prepare a large fish for canning in less than a minute.
The "Iron Chink," introduced toward the end of the nineteenth
century, automatically dressed the fish by decapitating it and
removing the entrails, tails, and fins, and preparing it for cutting into sections and placing in cans. Later came machines
producing double-seamed cans, thus eliminating the need to
seal the tops with acid and solder. Tin was imported from Eng-

TABLE 2
AVERAGE ANNUAL COLUMBIA RIVER CANNED SALMON PACK, 1866–1964
(cases in standard units of 48 pounds net weight)

Years	Chinook	Sockeye	Coho	Chum	Steelhead	Total
1866–70	60,000	. . .	. . .	. . .	. . .	60,000
1871–75	285,000	. . .	. . .	. . .	. . .	285,000
1876–80	460,000	. . .	. . .	. . .	. . .	460,000
1881–85	579,000	. . .	. . .	. . .	. . .	579,000
1886–90	356,000	15,000*	. . .	. . .	14,000*	385,000
1891–95	357,000	35,000	35,000†	5,000‡	54,000	486,000
1896–1900	330,000	27,000	49,000	6,000	51,000	463,000
1901–05	305,000	12,000	20,000	17,000	9,000	363,000
1906–10	237,000	11,000	43,000	32,000	9,000	332,000
1911–15	303,000	13,000	51,000	44,000	13,000	424,000
1916–20	402,000	12,000	66,000	51,000	19,000	550,000
1921–25	288,000	18,000	90,000	31,000	21,000	448,000
1926–30	282,000	11,000	84,000	58,000	24,000	459,000
1931–35	244,000	4,000	56,000	17,000	15,000	336,000
1936–40	228,000	12,000	61,000	28,000	22,000	351,000
1941–45	206,000	12,000	21,000	43,000	22,000	304,000
1946–50	183,000	8,000	27,000	17,000	16,000	251,000
1951–55	105,000	6,000	23,000	11,000	16,000	161,000
1956–60	80,000	19,000	16,000	5,000	8,000	128,000
1961–64	55,000	2,000	23,000	4,000	6,000	90,000

SOURCE: Pruter, "Commercial Fisheries of the Columbia River and Adjacent Ocean Waters."
*No pack before 1889.
†No pack before 1892.
‡No pack before 1893.

land. Finally came automatic filling, vacuum sealing, and labeling machines. By 1910 a cannery could pack 2,000 cases (96,000 one-pound cans) in ten hours for less than what 800 cases had formerly cost.

In addition to canning, part of the salmon catch was salted or mild cured for direct consumption. Prior to 1923 almost the entire mild-cure (lightly salted) packs consisted of chinook, and as much as 5 million pounds per year went to this part of the market. Completion of the transcontinental railway to Portland in 1883 made possible the shipment of salted fish to metropolitan areas in the East, Middle West, and Pacific Coast; the development of mechanical refrigeration enabled shippers to send frozen salmon to markets throughout the United States and Europe.

Astoria

When Mont Hawthorne, who worked in fish canneries most of his life, in Oregon and Alaska, began his career in Astoria in 1883 it was mostly a city built on pilings. "The streets was made like big wooden bridges," he says in his memoirs as related to Martha Ferguson McKeown.[1] Wooden canneries lined the waterfront, and close to each was the bunkhouse for the Chinese workers. It was a wild frontier town where men were kidnapped on the streets and sold to ship captains needing sailors for their vessels. Hawthorne says, "They'd knock a man right down on the street and take him out and sell him on a ship" (p. 7), and he would never be seen again. In the streets pigtailed Chinese wearing black blouses and soft shoes, Finns, Nowegians, Danes, and other nationalities jostled each other during the fishing season, which lasted from April to October. There were many dance halls, and a saloon on nearly every corner, each with a special attraction to lure customers. "If you didn't have the money, you could throw a big fresh salmon into a sort of a pen they had beside the ticket-taker and get in that way," says Hawthorne (p. 9). There was a red-light district and a miniature Chinatown where the merchants sold food and other things the Chinese liked. "Swilltown" was next to Chinatown and "every time the sailors hit the town they made a beeline for that section. So did the loggers and fishermen. George Hill had a stage. Girls danced there and got fellows to treat them and everybody else at the bar" (p. 11). Killings and robberies were everyday occurrences in Astoria at its peak of prosperity.

Cut off by its hinterland, Astoria could only be reached by boat. When Hawthorne went there in 1883 he had to go from Portland to San Francisco by train and there take a coastal steamer to Astoria. The wharves were crowded with fishing boats and cargo ships. Cases of salmon rolled from the canneries into the merchant ships destined for Liverpool, Valparaiso, New York, Honolulu.

The town had no sewer. Dead fish and offal were tossed into the river, and when the tide turned, the fish and offal drifted back to shore. Bears came out of the surrounding forest to gorge themselves on salmon while gulls attacked the rotting fish heads, entrails, and tails. In a banner year like 1889 every able-bodied person went fishing, including the pastors of the churches, so that Sunday services were canceled. Tons of fish the canneries could not handle in such a year were tossed overboard. "There wasn't no laws regulating what happened to the fish," says Hawthorne. "The fishermen tried to catch all they could. The canneries had agreed to take them. Each man tried to live up to his contract. Everyone aimed to make all he could. Folks in Astoria got pretty sore, but that was about the smell more than about the salmon being wasted" (p. 13).

Like all cannery towns up and down the Pacific Coast, Astoria declined as salmon supplies diminished and the industry shrank and eventually petered out. As table 1 shows, average annual commercial landings of salmon from the Columbia River dropped from 39.4 million pounds in 1881–85 to 26.1 million pounds in 1886–90; increased to 36.3 million pounds in the period 1911–15, reached an all-time high of 41.2 million pounds in 1916–20, and thereafter fell steadily as supplies decreased, especially after the high-dam era began with the completion of Rock Island Dam in 1933, Bonneville Dam in 1938, and Grand Coulee Dam in 1941. Average annual landings, excluding troll catches, were 34 million pounds in the 1920s, 23.5 million in the 1930s, 20 million in the 1940s, and only 9 million in the 1950s.

Only a few salmon canneries remain in the Astoria area and state of Oregon. Astoria is now a safe town. The Chinese have gone—there is not even a Chinese laundry left. Dance halls, gambling dens, and opium dens vanished long ago. The once impressive Astor Hotel has been intermittently closed. The steep streets topped by the faded Astor Column commemorating the city's founding by John Jacob Astor's Pacific Fur Company are filled with neat one-family homes. Few foreign ships now call at the port and the commercial fishing fleet has greatly diminished. Charter boats do a lively business taking tourists across the Columbia bar to troll for salmon at thirty-five to forty dollars a person each trip, not guaranteeing they will catch a fish. The economy depends largely on logging, sport fishing, and tourism.

The Canneries

To see what a Columbia River cannery was like let us betake ourselves to the Celilo Falls area where the Seufert family canned salmon from 1886 to 1954, developing the largest operation of its kind above Astoria (see Fig. 1).[2] F. A. Seufert and his brother Theodore started a fish cannery three miles east of The Dalles in 1885. The next year they built the first of many fish wheels on which much of their prosperity depended. These contraptions, which first appeared on the Columbia in 1879, are said to have been invented by the Williams brothers on models used in eastern rivers, notably in the shad fisheries on the Pee Dee and Roanoke rivers of North Carolina. There were two kinds of wheels on the river: stationary and floating. The stationary wheel was anywhere from 9 to 32 feet in diameter, activated by the current to attract and deposit the migrating fishes in a large bin on the shore. Some wheels had long leads of piling running out into the river, directing the fish into the wheel's range. The floating wheel was attached to a scow or barge, hence could be moved from one place to another as circumstances dictated, being anchored over a boil in the stream which served as attraction water. Salmon following the shore would be intercepted and caught. Like the gillnet, it was most successful in turbid water. Wheels worked best in narrow channels with fast currents, as around Celilo Falls.

The Seuferts obtained the bulk of their fish from the wheels until they were outlawed by the legislatures of Oregon in 1926 and Washington in 1934 under pressure of the netmen who regarded them as unfair competitors. The Seuferts also had many gillnetters fishing for them and purchased considerable amounts of fish from the Indian dipnetters who came to the reservation at Celilo each year. A few unemployed white men who took up fishing during the Depression dipnetted around the stationary wheels and sold their catches to the Seuferts.

In his memoirs, scheduled to be published by the Oregon Historical Society, Francis A. Seufert, last president of the Seufert Canning Company, says that at the peak of their operations they had eleven scows and five stationary wheels. In the flood year 1894, when the Columbia River was at its highest level in a century, nearly all the Seufert wheels were damaged with the exception of the Phelps wheel, which caught 227,000 pounds of salmon between May 17 and July 31, peaking at 42,000 pounds on July 2, mostly blueback. "As a result of its one phenomenal success," say Donaldson and Cramer in *Fishwheels of the Columbia*, "the Phelps dipper paid for the repair of all the remaining Seufert wheels damaged by the flood."[3] Wheel No. 5, however, was the big

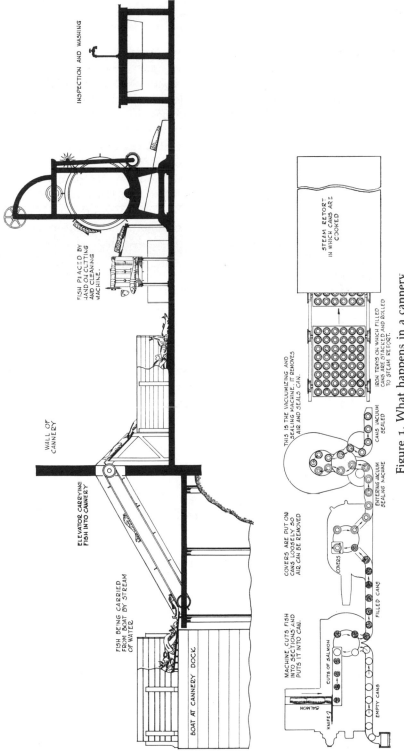

INSPECTION AND WASHING

FISH PLACED BY HAND ON CUTTING AND CLEANING MACHINE.

WALL OF CANNERY

ELEVATOR CARRYING FISH INTO CANNERY

FISH BEING CARRIED FROM BOAT BY STREAM OF WATER

BOAT AT CANNERY DOCK.

STEAM RETORT— IN WHICH CANS ARE COOKED

IRON TRAYS ON WHICH FILLED CANS ARE STACKED AND ROLLED TO STEAM RETORT.

THIS IS THE VACUUMIZING AND SEALING MACHINE. IT REMOVES AIR AND SEALS CAN.

CANS VACUUM SEALED

ENTERING VACUUM SEALING MACHINE

COVERS ARE PUT ON CANS LOOSELY SO AIR CAN BE REMOVED

COVERS

FILLED CANS

MACHINE CUTS FISH INTO SECTIONS AND PUTS IT INTO CAN.

CUTS OF SALMON

SALMON

KNIFE

EMPTY CANS

Figure 1. What happens in a cannery

moneymaker. "It caught more fish and made more money than any fish wheel on the Columbia River," says Seufert.

A wheel could take 40 to 50 tons of salmon in a season; it was cheap to operate, requiring only a watchman to guard it night and day to scare away robbers. It worked best in the early morning when the fish, having rested all night, began to move upstream through the treacherous narrow channel. The Seuferts also operated purse seines and kept a stable of horses to work them.

The main outlets for their canned salmon were eastern markets, especially New York City with its teeming East European Jewish immigrant population. A half-pound can of salmon or steelhead (sold as salmon) and buttered rye or pumpernickel bread made a solid and inexpensive luncheon for the sweatshop workers. In immigrant families like ours in Chicago, canned salmon was a popular food, sometimes made into fried cakes by my mother. We also enjoyed mild-cure salmon known as "lox" (the Yiddish word) spread on a buttered bagel. In the 1920s a one-pound can of salmon cost about 50 cents, and a half pound of lox 75 cents.

Columbia River salmon was also in great demand in the British Isles, especially in the working-class districts of the industrial cities. John West, one of the early canners, introduced it to England through the distributors Stanley and Pelling of Liverpool. They have retained the brand name John West to this day. At the turn of the century Stanley and Pelling were importing 250,000 cans of Oregon salmon a year, mainly from R. D. Hume, who had a monopoly on the rich Rogue River fishery.

The typical Columbia River cannery was a long, rambling structure like the Seuferts' which stood on a bluff overlooking the river on the Oregon side. The labor force was entirely Chinese except for the engineer, cook, and maintenance personnel. "The Chinese," says Francis Seufert, "were bachelors, living in their own bunkhouse known as the Chinee House. They had few or no relatives or friends at The Dalles (the nearest town). They only associated with each other. Their whole world revolved around the company. Their bunkhouse was a wooden structure where each person had his own room furnished with an iron bed but no mattress. They would only sleep on boards. If you put springs and mattresses in the Chinee house you would find them outside the next morning. They had their own Chinese cook who prepared all their meals, consisting of rice, Chinese vegetables, duck or pork. They liked pastries and every day the grocery truck or wagon would come out from The Dalles to supply them with pastries for which they paid themselves—the company paid for all the other food and lodging."

The crew was recruited by a Chinese grocery store in Portland who also supplied the Chinese with the food and supplies they needed. "You went to Portland and bought tickets for fifty men," says Seufert, "notified the railroad what day they were to leave and a special car was hooked onto the regular train to bring them to the cannery at Seufert Station along with their luggage which consisted of a three-gallon bucket for each man, containing his clothes and other personal belongings. In the Chinee house it served as a suitcase and also a bathtub because he could take a sponge bath from the bucket. All the men belonged to the same Tong, else there might be a war in the Chinee house and you would wake up some morning with a lot of dead Chinamen on your hands."

In the cannery the Chinese took orders only from the China boss (none of them could speak English): "You told them what you wanted done and he gave the orders and saw that they were carried out. . . . You also had to supply them with a Chinese cook and bookkeeper, provide them with pigs and ducks which we bought from local farmers. The men raised them all summer and butchered them as they were needed."

The labor contract ran from April 25 to October 15. Until World War I they worked twelve hours a day, Monday through Saturday, 6 A.M. to 6 P.M., with an hour off for lunch. In the 1920s this was reduced to ten hours and in the 1930s to eight hours a day, with extra pay for overtime. There was no workmen's compensation for injuries on the job, or unemployment insurance or social security deductions to which the firm had to contribute.

The men were paid off on the last day of the season in a lump sum, usually in large bills: "You then went down to The Dalles, bought tickets for the entire crew, notified the railroad and the passenger train was flagged at Seufert station the day they were returning to Portland, still dressed in silk blouses and silk trousers, as silent and unemotional as when they came."

The Seufert Canning Company went out of business in 1954, as The Dalles Dam was about to be completed. The U.S. government paid the company $600,000 for its property and fishing rights.

In the Portland *Oregonian* of August 2, 1970, there was an interview with the last of the China bosses, Kee Brown, who came to Astoria in 1902 as a baby strapped to his mother's back. "I learned the canning business from the ground up," he told the reporter. "Give me tin, acid and a soldering iron and I can still make a salmon can. In those days the season began in April, when the Chinese arrived from Canton, Seattle, Portland or San Francisco. We had as many as 125 in a crew. There was never any written agreement between the contractor and the workers, only with the cannery. We got 48¢ for each case of salmon (1¢ per can) ready for shipment. Salmon was then selling for $4.00 a case. We paid the men $15 a month. They were fed and lodged at the company's expense. The canneries guaranteed the contractors so many cases a season, and in good fishing years we made money."

At sixty-nine Kee Brown was still associated with the canning industry. "The past sixty years in Astoria have been good to Kee," said the reporter. "He fathered six sons and two daughters who grew up to be good American citizens." His father, who brought him to the United States from Canton, lies buried in a cemetery east of Astoria beside the wife whose bound feet did not prevent her from following her husband across the Pacific to make his living exploiting his fellow countrymen under a system of coolie labor.

A Plethora of Gear

In the heyday of the fishery every conceivable type of gear was seen on the Columbia. Control of fishing such as existed in some European countries was then unwanted in the United States, and regulations on the statute books were generally flouted. Americans thought they could help themselves to whatever public resources they wanted without restraint—fish, timber, wildlife, water, and so on. The major kinds of gear were gillnets, purse seines, traps (pounds like those employed in Maine to deplete its salmon runs), wheels, dipnets, set nets, and troll lines. The Columbia River was packed with floating and fixed gear from Astoria to The Dalles, around the Deschutes River, on the Willamette below the falls, on the Clackamas, and some netsmen were even working the lowest seventy miles of the Snake River.

The earliest gillnets were adopted from the Indians. Hapgood, Hume and Company operated two of these around Eagle Cliff, each 125 fathoms long (750 feet) and 23 feet deep. These nets were constantly enlarged until by 1880 they were 300 to 350 fathoms long with a mesh of 8 inches. Mesh sizes were reduced as chinook runs declined and smaller fish (sockeye, steelhead, chum, and silvers) were harvested. The gillnet is essentially a rectangular piece of webbing paid out from a boat, drifting with the current (see Fig. 2). Fish jam their heads through the mesh

Figure 2. Gillnetter

openings and are hopelessly trapped. The cork line keeps the net afloat while the lead line at the bottom pulls the webbing down into the water. In turbid water the fish moving upstream head straight into the net (which they cannot see). A gillnet boat may be operated by one or two persons. Early gillnet boats were moved by sails or oars; later ones were equipped with gasoline engines and a "gurdy" for hauling in the net. Gillnets were also anchored at a fixed location: these are called set nets.

A distinctive type of "Columbia River boat" became associated with gillnetting and was widely adopted on the Pacific coast, notably in Alaska. At first it was 22 to 23 feet long and entirely open. By 1880 washboards were added with small deck spaces at the end. Ordinarily it had a single sprit sail and occasionally a jib as well as oars used to overcome the currents and tides. Every boat had a small stove and larder of provisions. By 1889 some 2,600 rowboats and sailboats were pursuing the salmon in the river from Portland to the mouth, belonging to what boatmen call the "mosquito fleet." When gasoline engines became available, gillnetting became much more efficient. By 1915 the commercial fishing fleet was almost fully motorized. Until about 1935, drift gillnets were the most important type of gear in the number of units employed and size of catch. According to Craig and Hacker, in their *History and Development of the Fisheries of the Columbia River,* they took 83 percent of the chinook, 5 percent of the chum, 5 percent of the steelhead, and smaller proportions of the silvers and sockeye catches.[4]

Seines, introduced by the Indians, were adopted by the white men and made larger and more efficient. A seine consists of a large net, one edge provided with sinkers and the other with floats. It hangs vertically in the water, and when the ends are drawn together, like a purse, or drawn ashore, it encloses the fish. Lines are attached to both ends. On the Columbia the seines, laid out from skiffs, were pulled by horses. They required an average crew of twenty-four men. Some of the horses, says Stewart Holbrook in his book *The Columbia,* "were often played-out relics of the Portland streetcar system, later veterans of the fire department." Seine nets ranged from 100 to 400 fathoms with a bunt or bag 50 fathoms long in the central part which enclosed the fish. Seining was confined to the area below Celilo Falls, being most effective on the low sandy spits, islands, and tidal areas. Development of hydraulic power eliminated the horses.

In Baker's Bay on the Washington side of the Columbia, fishermen planted pound nets along the shore until the area from Canby to Point Ellice was virtually barricaded with them. Angry gillnetters sometimes made night raids on these traps, cutting the mooring lines and setting them adrift. Terrorized watchmen were helpless. These intermittent fish wars lasted until all stationary gear except setnets (used by Indians) was declared illegal in both Washington and Oregon.

As the salmon fishery spread upriver, fish buyers established stations close to the best fishing grounds so that fishermen could deliver their catches to them promptly. Usually at these stations, like Corbett below Bonneville, a hamlet grew up consisting of a restaurant featuring fresh salmon, a tavern, and—when automobiles became common—a gas station and repair shop. These buying stations disappeared as the river fishery declined, but as late as 1958 the Corbett station was still in use.

When dependable gasoline motors replaced sails, many fishermen moved out to the open sea to troll for salmon, a technique which was also known to the Indians who trolled inside the river

from canoes. Trolling is by hook and line, and is an effective
method for taking chinook and coho salmon (see Fig. 3). It was

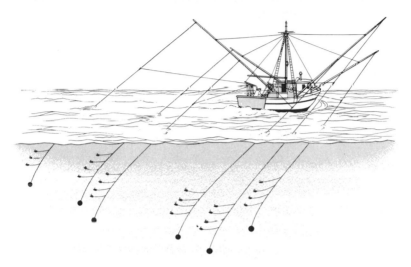

Figure 3. Troller

started around 1912 by Norwegian immigrants who discovered
they could catch more fish outside the river at certain times of the
year with this gear than by netting in the river. The motorized
trolling fleet swelled to over a thousand by 1920, after which the
number declined.

A troller "ordinarily has two poles on each side," say Craig and
Hacker in *History and Development of the Fisheries of the Columbia River*,
"either hinged so that they can be pulled up into a vertical position
or fitted into sockets so that they can be removed inboard when
not in use" (p. 181). When fishing one or two lines, hooks are
attached to each pole and the poles are extended out from the side
of the boat. Since the fish in the ocean are still feeding, the hooks
are baited with herring or pilchards and adorned with colorful
spoons or spinners and the lines weighted down with lead sinkers.
Trolling can be very dangerous: gales and hurricanes come up
without warning. Every fishing port on the Oregon and Washington coast has seen trollers leave the little harbor in the morning in
a calm sea and never return. Sometimes the bodies of the fishermen are found, but more often they disappear in the deep and are

never recovered. In the days before loran and radiotelephone the losses were much greater than they are today, especially because there were no really adequate lifesaving services or weather warnings. At first trollers could only go 25 miles out to sea and 45 to 50 miles north or south of the Columbia River. With improved internal combustion engines, their boats have a wide cruising radius and can stay out for days.

Now only trolling is permitted for salmon seaward of the river's mouth and only gillnetting in the rivers except for sportsmen, who are allowed to troll or angle in the rivers and troll offshore. It is a pleasant sight to see the trollers return from the fishing grounds at the end of the day, to such ports as Warrenton, Garibaldi, Depoe Bay, Newport, and Astoria, Oregon, their poles up, slowly heading for the docks as the sun sets behind them and the sea turns crimson. In these towns one may buy salmon fresh from the boat, or dine in a restaurant that serves fresh salmon, a meal fit for a king.

Failure of Regulation

Armadas of fishing boats jammed the lower Columbia in the days of sail and later, so that it seemed at times one could walk across the river on their decks. The furious pace of exploitation was not confined to the Columbia: it occurred on the Sacramento, the Fraser, and many other streams from Bristol Bay to Monterey Bay rich in salmon. Demand was inexhaustible, and the fishermen, packers, and fish merchants making handsome profits were determined to satisfy it, and defy the authorities if necessary.

Timid efforts were made in the early days of the fishery by state and territorial governments to impose some kind of restraints. In 1871 Washington Territory declared it unlawful "to build or place a fish-trap, weir, seine or net two-thirds of the way across fresh water streams, creeks or lakes, if it would prevent the passage of fish either up or down." Oregon followed suit two decades later. In 1878 Oregon issued regulations specifying minimum net sizes and spacing between slats or traps, and requiring traps and weirs to have openings permitting the free passage of fish during weekly closed periods. In 1897 Washington, now a state, passed similar legislation.[5]

In 1893 Washington for the first time specified the maximum allowable length of fixed gear on the river and the minimum distance between them. Oregon refrained from imposing such restrictions, and in the light of the difficulty of enforcing any controls on fishing because the legislature refused to appropriate more than a pittance for enforcement, this seemed altogether wise.

Regulation of fishing seasons began in 1877 when Washington closed the Columbia to fishing during March, April, August, and September with additional weekend closures (Saturday 6 P.M. to Sunday 6 P.M.) in May, June, and July in order to enhance the escapement. Oregon followed suit the next year but omitted the April closure. Over the next three decades this pattern of closure remained on the statute books. Since little was known about the size of the runs and not much more about the biology of anadromous fishes—neither state had any biologists working on fish problems—management, such as it was, operated in the dark. Moreover, the states did not correlate their regulations as they do now. For practical purposes the statutes were really dead letters.

Oregon created a Board of Fish Commissioners in 1887, and Washington a Fish Commission in 1890. In its first *Report to the Governor* (1889) the Oregon board reported that "the greatest difficulty in enforcing the laws is the lack of funds. As fishing is carried on from the mouth of the Columbia to Celilo, a distance of over 200 miles, and from the mouth of the Willamette to its falls, a distance of 25 miles, and up the Clackamas for 20 miles, and most of the fishing being done during the night, you will plainly see that it is impossible for one man or even three to see that the law is enforced at all points at the same time. In order that the literal law may be enforced it would be necessary to station a river police at the principal centers." This was not done.

Whatever enforcement there was was confined to the most flagrant and easily caught offenders, and few of them were brought to court. The Oregon Board of Fish Commissioners said in its first report, "In regard to the weekly close time, we will say that this part of the law had it been enforced would have fallen entirely on the fishermen, and owing to the heavy fine of $500, or one year's imprisonment, we were advised by good authority not to enforce this part of the law." Only one man was available who "could attend to the enforcement of the law regarding the close time of August and September"; here "the commission did all they could . . . and met with much better success than we anticipated."

A weakness of the law, the board complained in its second report (1891), was that "it does not prohibit the common carrier from receiving and transporting fresh salmon during the close times; if it did the law could be more easily enforced. . . . No one seems to know if a steelhead, blueback or silverside [coho] is a salmon under the law or not. A person may catch any of these varieties during the close time and deem they are not salmon."

The first report of the Oregon Fish and Game Protector (1894), who replaced the Board of Fish Commissioners, reveals what unrestrained fishing and failure of regulation accomplished:

> It does not require a study of the statistics to convince one that the salmon industry has suffered a great decline during the past decade, and that it is only a matter of a few years under present conditions when the chinook of the Columbia will be as scarce as the beaver that once was so plentiful in our streams. Common observance is amply able to apprehend a fact so plain. For a third of a century Oregon has drawn wealth from her streams, but now, by reason of her wastefulness and lack of intelligent provision for the future, the source of that wealth is disappearing and is threatened with annihilation. . . . Salmon that ten years ago the canners would not touch now constitute 30 to 40 percent of the pack.

Such warnings were to be sounded by men in positions of authority again and again in the next half century, especially after the people of the Pacific Northwest were lulled into the belief that the great rivers could be honeycombed with multipurpose dams without seriously affecting the salmon and steelhead runs.

In 1917 John W. Cobb wrote in the annual report of the U.S. Bureau of Fisheries: "When the enormous number of fishermen engaged and the immense quantity of gear employed is considered, one sometimes wonders how many of the fish, in certain streams at least, escape."

In analyzing the 1938 Columbia River runs Willis H. Rich, director of research of the Oregon Fish Commission, attributed the decline to an escapement "well below the level that would provide the maximum sustained yield." He pointed out that "such regulations and restrictions as have been imposed upon the Columbia River salmon fisheries apparently have very little effect insofar as they may act to reduce the intensity of fishing and provide a greater escapement." He regarded the weekend closure as of little value from the standpoint of conservation, while the beneficial effects of the closed season on the lower river (August 25 to September 20) were largely offset by intensive fishing during September and October above Bonneville. He concluded that "on the whole, it would appear the chinook salmon runs [which then constituted a substantial portion of the total catches] are subjected to an exceedingly intense fishery without any effective protection whatsoever, except such as has been afforded by the elimination of certain forms of gear and artificial propagation."[6]

CHAPTER 4

Life History
of the Salmon and Steelhead Trout

My acquaintance with the Columbia River salmon began on a
warm and sunny autumnal morning in 1952 when my boss Dr.
Paul Raver, administrator of the Bonneville Power Administration, sent me to view the fish ladders at Bonneville Dam in connec-
tion with a study I was making of the impact of the dams on the
salmon runs. At that time, when there were only a few dams on
the main stem of the Columbia and none on the Snake River below
Swan Falls, Congress was loath to authorize any more federal
multipurpose projects on these rivers unless it was convinced that
salmon could be passed over them in adequate numbers. Before
this visit, having lived in the East all my life, I had never seen a
salmon dead or alive, although when I was a child our family ate
plenty of canned and mild-cure salmon, then inexpensive and
nutritious food.

As I stood beside the fish ladder on Bradford Island, mesmer-
ized by the sleek, torpedo-shaped fishes attempting to climb the
steeplechase man had placed in their path, a series of curving,
stepped-up pools down which powerful jets of water created an
artificial attraction current, I wondered why they were so determined to climb this hurdle and reach the counting-board where a
lady sitting in a hut ticked them off on a hand counter as they
passed into the reservoir. They quickly sped upstream.

I wondered whither they were going, and where they had come
from. I then knew little of their life history. In the next twenty
years I learned a great deal about them as I trekked around the
world trying to unravel their mysteries. The fish I had seen that
morning at the dam may have paid visits to the west coast of
Vancouver Island where there were rich ocean pastures, or perhaps
had gone farther north to the Queen Charlotte Islands, another

important feeding ground, or ventured still farther to the Gulf of Alaska. As to where they were now going upstream, all one could say is that they were attempting to reach natal waters where they would spawn and nowhere else—perhaps in the mid-Columbia region, northern Washington, or the Snake River tributaries in Idaho.

The questions multiplied in the course of my research: what kind of clues do the salmon use in their extensive migrations in the ocean? Do they take measurements from the sun and moon as perhaps birds do? Or do they "feel" their way over routes of thousands of miles by means of electromagnetic currents? Do they have built-in clocks that tell them when it is time to cease their wanderings and race for home? How do they find their home rivers, as they usually do unerringly, in seas that have no landmarks? The answers to these questions led to other questions until from reading and travel, talking to biologists, fishermen, and others working on salmon problems, I unraveled much of their life history, though much remains unknown. No group of fishes has inspired more research into their behavior and life history than the salmon.

Freshwater or Marine Origin?

The origin of the anadromous life of the salmon, spent partly in fresh water and partly in the ocean, has aroused considerable speculation since Konrad von Gesner in the sixteenth century first accurately described it. Were they originally freshwater species, like trout, grayling, and bass, or did they originate as marine species?

The ichthyologist Albert Günther, author of the encyclopedic *Catalogue of Fishes in the British Museum* (1859–70), argued that the salmon and seagoing trout like steelhead are freshwater fishes which in their evolution acquired the habit of going to sea to feed and returning to the safe haven of the rivers to spawn. A contrary view was expressed by the eminent British ichthyologist Francis Day in 1867, namely, that they originated in a remote geologic era as marine fishes but developed the habit of entering the rivers for the purpose of spawning and rearing their young. Today the latter view has few supporters, if any.

Professor J. M. Macfarlane, in his book *The Evolution and Distribution of Fishes* (1923), says, "Against the possible marine ancestry for

Salmonidae many grave objections can be urged. . . . It is difficult to imagine genera like *Salmo* . . . which show few or no truly marine species, becoming dispersed as they are over land areas of the northern hemisphere, if they were marine—or even coastal— derivatives. A considerable number, further, show the anadromous or 'homing instinct,' in that though often migrating seaward to feed, they return to rivers or lakes to spawn. . . . The swim-bladder also is highly developed in primitive and freshwater types, but gradually becomes small and even absorbed in marine species. These with other strong reasons compel the writer to accept a freshwater origin for the family to which salmon and trout belong."[1]

The late Russian ichthyologist G. V. Nikolsky agreed with Macfarlane. According to him, the change from a freshwater to a migratory life was made easy by the dilution of the seas that occurred about a million years ago in the Northern Hemisphere when an enormous mass of fresh water significantly reduced the salinity of parts of the ocean in areas adjacent to glaciated lands, forcing the freshwater fishes to seek their food in the sea. As time passed, some of the Salmonidae began to migrate longer distances in the ocean to find their pastures but invariably returned to the home streams. Here they spawned and died and their offspring carried on the anadromous way of life.[2] This process of natural selection, which included several mutations, separated many of the anadromous from the resident species of Salmonidae and occurred over a long period of time, probably several hundred thousand years.

The Pacific Species

The Pacific salmon, belonging to the genus *Oncorhynchus* (which means hooked snout), are unique among Salmonidae in many respects, especially in the size of some species and the extensive migrations they undertake.

The five species found in North America are listed below (see also Fig. 4):

Oncorhynchus tshawytscha, largest in size, is known as chinook in Oregon and king in California, Washington, British Columbia, and Alaska. It is also called quinnat (the Indian name), tyee (an Indian word meaning chief), and Sacramento salmon. Its range is from the Bering Sea to Monterey Bay. The Columbia River

STEELHEAD TROUT

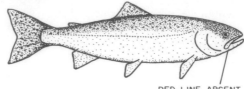

RED LINE ABSENT

CHINOOK SALMON

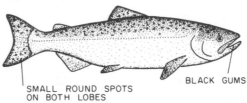

SMALL ROUND SPOTS
ON BOTH LOBES

BLACK GUMS

COHO SALMON

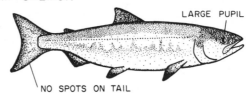

SMALL ROUND SPOTS
ON UPPER LOBE ONLY

WHITE GUMS

CHUM SALMON

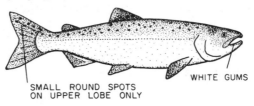

LARGE PUPIL

NO SPOTS ON TAIL

SOCKEYE SALMON

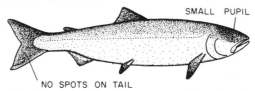

SMALL PUPIL

NO SPOTS ON TAIL

Figure 4. The steelhead trout and the four species of Pacific salmon native
to the Columbia River (source: Somerton and Murray, *Field Guide to the Fish
of Puget Sound and the Northwest Coast*)

watershed originally contained more chinook than any other river system in the world.

O. nerka is the red salmon of Alaska, supreme for canning, the sockeye of British Columbia and Puget Sound, and blueback of the Columbia River. Landlocked forms of dwarf size are known as kokanee, kickaninny, or little redfish, found in some of the lakes in the Columbia drainage. Sockeye hatch mainly in streams with access to adjoining lakes in which the juveniles are reared. Many sockeye rivers became derelict when the lakes were barricaded by irrigation dams.

O. kisutch, known as coho, silvers, or silversides in the Columbia River, Puget Sound, and British Columbia, were present originally in many of the accessible streams emptying into the Pacific from the Bering Strait to the Sacramento River.

O. keta, chum or dog salmon, originally plentiful in Oregon's coastal rivers and the Columbia, is found in abundance in streams emptying into Puget Sound, and in British Columbia and Alaska.

O. gorbuscha, distinguished by the humpback of the mature male, is the pink salmon, also called humpy, of Alaska, British Columbia, and Puget Sound, but is not native to the Columbia River, although strays may occur.

Russian names are attached to the five species because they were first identified by Russian naturalists in the eighteenth century who explored the Far Eastern provinces where they are found. A sixth species, *O. masu,* the cherry salmon of Japan, Korea, and Russia, does not occur in North America.

Steelhead trout, *Salmo gairdneri,* is a sea-run rainbow trout with many of the biological characteristics of the salmon, including the habit of spending much of its life in the ocean and returning to the rivers to spawn. Morphologically it is closer to the Atlantic salmon *(Salmo salar)* than to the *Oncorhynchus* species. Like the Atlantic salmon, some steelhead may recover from spawning and return to the sea; all Pacific salmon die after this ordeal. The Columbia River watershed is the world's greatest producer of steelhead trout.

Table 3 summarizes the biological characteristics of the different Columbia River species.

TABLE 3

LIFE HISTORY OF THE COLUMBIA RIVER SALMON AND STEELHEAD TROUT

	Oncorhynchus tshawytscha	O. nerka	O. kisutch	O. keta	Salmo gairdneri
Common Names	Chinook King (Alaska and California) Quinnat (New Zealand)	Sockeye Blueback Red (Alaska)	Coho Silver Silverside	Chum Dog	Steelhead trout
Length of Freshwater Life	Fall chinook: few days to 4 months Spring chinook: 1 to 2 years	1 or more years	1 to 2 years	Few days	Generally 1 to 3 years
Length of Ocean Life	1 to 5 years (generally 2 to 3)	1 to 4 years	Generally 1 to 1.5 years	1 to 5 years	1 to 3 years
Average Length at Maturity	28 to 36 inches	19 to 21 inches	26 to 28 inches	27 to 29 inches	27 to 29 inches
Average Weight at Maturity	15 to 25 pounds	3 to 5 pounds	7 to 9 pounds	11 to 12 pounds	9 to 10 pounds
Range of Weight at Maturity	2.5 to 90 pounds	2 to 12 pounds	1.5 to 30 pounds	3 to 36 pounds	3 to 37 pounds
Principal Spawning Months	August-December	August-October	September-February	October-December	December-June
Fecundity of Female (average number of eggs)	5,000	3,500	3,000	2,500 to 3,000	3,000 to 4,000

Life in the River

Salmon begin life as fertilized pinkish eggs about the size of buckshot buried in the gravel of a swift-flowing stream. There they remain for varying periods of time, depending upon water temperatures. Chinook eggs hatch out in about 50 days in water of 50 degrees F. The alevin, as the larvae are called, are translucent fishes with black eyes and spotted backs, about an inch long, and are attached to a large yolk sac which provides their initial nourishment; when the sac is absorbed, they emerge as fry from the gravel bed and begin to forage for food. Pinks, chum, and sometimes other salmon species descend to the sea in the fry stage. The young of those chinook that enter the Columbia River in the fall (fall chinook) tend to stay in the river from a few to 120 days after emergence from the redds, while the young of spring chinook remain a year or more before descending to the ocean. Young sockeye spend a year or two before leaving the lakes and descending to the sea. Young coho in the Columbia generally spend one year in fresh water while young steelhead stay about two years.

In the river a plethora of food is available to these tiny fishes: crustaceans, insects, mollusks, annelid worms, and others. Growth is quickest in summer, when food is abundant, and slower in winter. Water temperatures also affect the rate of growth: colder temperatures slow down growth, and warmer than optimum temperatures may cause pathological problems.

The first year of life is the most precarious. The eggs may be washed out by flood waters; they are sought by bottom organisms like crayfish and aquatic insects. Fry are eaten by larger fish, other juvenile salmon and trout, squawfish, crayfish, birds, and even snakes. Squawfish, whose population has multiplied in the Columbia River since it has been dammed and converted into a chain of reservoirs, account for a considerable mortality of young salmon.

After the fry stage comes the fingerling and finally the smolt stage when the fishes migrate downstream and adapt themselves to life in the ocean. Marked physiological changes occur before they enter the marine environment. They acquire a silvery coat, scales become prominent and can be easily rubbed off, tails lengthen and become more deeply forked. Just before they start their seaward migration they become more buoyant as the swim bladder is enlarged. Salmon fingerlings are 2 to 6 inches long.

The tiny fishes descend in stages, in shoals, heads facing upstream, the water pouring into their mouths and passing through the gills. The current carries them down, from the headwaters to the sea, sometimes encompassing a journey of many hundreds of miles; when it slackens they turn and actively swim. Before Grand Coulee Dam was built many juvenile spring chinook and sockeye had to go over a thousand miles to reach the sea, and the adults made the same journey on their return.

In the headwaters of the rivers there is an enormous stirring in April and May as the hordes of young salmon and steelhead start their downstream migration. Some rivers send down millions of little fishes. They come into the Columbia from every corner of the watershed, from rivers, lakes, creeks, and streamlets. Nothing can stop them for the sea is their home. In the estuary they linger long enough to become familiar with the chemical cues of the water so they will recognize them through their olfactory sense upon their return two, three, or four years later. This process is called "imprinting."

Timing of the migration depends on changes in light and temperature as well as water flow. Spring spates alert the smolts. They travel mostly between dusk and dawn, when they are invisible to aerial predators, moving at a pace of up to five miles a day, sliding over rocks, down precipices, occasionally snapping at a fly, eating greedily. Some streams offer obstacles in the form of moving rafts of undecomposed sewage or other organic wastes. In the Columbia and Snake rivers, the highways to the ocean, they are now confronted by a series of gigantic dams which can be passed only by going through the swiftly revolving blades of the turbines at the powerhouses or over the fearsome spillways.

"Where does this memory of sea water, inherited by the little fishes from their parents, reside?" asks Louis Roule in his book *Fishes: Their Journeys and Migrations.* "And how does it come into existence in the little creatures who still only know the fugitive, flowing waters of their native torrent?" Scientists have attempted to answer these questions by means of intensive tagging experiments which show that no matter where the salmon or steelhead wander, they invariably find their way home. For instance, marked fishes tagged around Adak in the Aleutian Islands, identified as Columbia River salmon, were subsequently recovered in their native stream over two thousand miles away. That they follow predetermined routes, extending sometimes over half the north Pacific, is now known. Their itineraries, it is believed, are imprinted on their chromosomes. Their schedule is almost as exact as an ocean liner's.

Only a tiny fraction of the fishes that hatch out in the gravel survive to reach the sea. Dr. R. E. Foerster, who spent a lifetime studying the sockeye in British Columbia, offers a hypothetic survival table based on data from several Canadian rivers and lakes. Assuming that 1,000 adults enter the river, 500 males and 500 females each bearing 4,000 eggs (a total of 2,000,000), their fate under normal conditions may be as follows:

1. Ninety-five percent of the adults will survive the migration to the spawning grounds, leaving 1,900,000 eggs.
2. There will be a 50 percent loss of eggs, leaving 950,000 to be incubated and become alevins.
3. Seventy-five percent of the alevins will be killed during emergence from the redds and while migrating from the rivers into the lakes where young sockeye are reared, resulting in about 237,000 fry.
4. About 92 percent of the fry will die, leaving some 17,000 fingerlings to make the journey to the sea.[3]

How this ratio applies to species other than sockeye, and under abnormal conditions such as the conversion of the Columbia into a series of slack-water lakes above Bonneville, we do not know. However, in some recent years up to 90 percent of the fingerlings issuing from the Snake River watershed never reached the ocean. In addition, many adult fish leaving the ocean die on the way to the spawning grounds.

In order to maintain a stable population in a given river, without adding hatchery stock, every pair of adults who mate must produce at least one pair of offspring who will survive all the hazards of their juvenile and adult lives, including evasion of fishermen's nets, traps, and hooks, and return to the river to spawn successfully. If this ratio is not maintained, the run will decline, and may eventually peter out unless augmented by hatchery stock. This has happened to chinook and other upriver races in the Columbia.

Life in the Ocean

The ocean remains for us, as for the ancient Greeks who scarcely ever sailed beyond the Mediterranean Sea, the most mysterious part of the planet, despite such ingenious explorations as those of Jacques Cousteau and his colleagues. In its depths dwell multifarious creatures of infinite shapes and biological characteristics, a dazzling world which the salmon enter when they disappear from our view. Slowly we are unraveling some of the secrets of their life in the sea, but much remains tantalizingly unknown.

One of the critical periods in the fishes' existence occurs when they plunge into the ocean. "Since several freshwater functions are contrary to their marine counterparts," says Professor Lynwood Smith of the College of Fisheries of the University of Washington, "optimum adjustment is impossible during the period. Additional stress such as high temperatures, low oxygen levels in the water, pollutants . . . further complicates the situation and can lead to fatal consequences. And finally, in the sea a number of other changes—new food to recognize and catch, different predators to avoid and unknown large bodies of water to traverse. It's a rough transition."[4]

They start ocean life as plankton feeders and as they develop strong jaws and sharp teeth are enabled to devour microcrustaceans such as krill and shrimp (which are said to give the salmon their pinkish flesh), anchovies, pilchards, and small herring. Typical of the food found in chinook caught at sea are sand lance and anchovy, with herring and pilchard being most common. Predators are numerous: remains of salmon have been recovered from the stomachs of various marine fishes, pollock, tuna, whiting, swordfish, and seals that hover around bays and estuaries.

The salmon follow their food supply wherever it leads them, but individuals take various courses, for reasons unfathomable. Why do some juvenile chinook and coho after crossing the Columbia bar go northward and others southward? Why do some travel as far as the Aleutians to feed and others stay fairly close to the Oregon coast or journey to the Farallon Islands 35 miles west of the Golden Gate?

The routes of the salmon in the ocean have been extensively tracked by biologists. Before the smolts or fingerlings leave the rivers they are captured and marked for identification by imbedding a coded wire in the nose, or by removing a fin or two, or stamping or tattooing them with a number or symbol in fluorescent ink so that when recovered the wire or part of the fish will be returned to the address given. Hundreds of thousands of salmon, both juveniles and matures, have been tagged, and numerous recaptures tell us about their amazing travels. Tagged Columbia River salmon and steelhead have been caught off the Aleutian Islands, the Queen Charlotte Islands, the Oregon coast, and northern California. These have come from commercial and sport fishermen and from American, Canadian, and Japanese research vessels.

Until fairly recent years the ocean life of the steelhead was quite obscure. But now tagging experiments offer clues as to where they go. Many do not journey beyond the continental shelf but hang around coastal waters for one winter and return to the rivers weighing as little as one-half to two pounds. Others vie with chinook, sockeye, and pink salmon for long-distance honors. A steelhead tagged southeast of Adak Island on July 19, 1958, was hooked by an angler on the Chehalis River, Washington, ten months later, a trek of at least 2,000 miles. Another steelhead tagged south of Kodiak, Alaska, on August 8, 1958, was recaptured in the Samish River, Washington, over 1,000 miles away, eight months later. A steelhead tagged as a smolt on the Stillaguamish River, which empties into Puget Sound, wound up in the gillnet of a Japanese research vessel fifteen months later near Adak Island, about 2,000 miles distant. More astonishing is the steelhead captured and tagged by a research team around Adak which was recovered in the Salmon River, Idaho, having traveled possibly 3,000 miles to reach its home stream.[5]

Columbia River chinook and coho are taken in large numbers by trollers off the coasts of California, Washington, British Columbia, and Alaska. They have been caught as far north as Baranof Island, Alaska. The general movement of these fishes is in a counterclockwise direction until they are ready to come home. Very little is known about the migrations of the Columbia River sockeye, but sockeye are among the greatest of anadromous marine voyagers: fish from Bristol Bay, Alaska, are known to pay calls on the waters around the Kamchatka Peninsula in Siberia, mingle with Russian salmon, and complete orbits of up to 10,000 miles before returning to their home rivers.

Since all Pacific salmon die after spawning, none of the fishes swimming in shoals in the cresting seas have yet spawned, but there may be steelhead among them that are on their second and in a few cases their third or even fourth round trip. Donald Chapman, in his report "The Life History of the Alsea River Steelhead," says that 17 percent of the 1954 run into that river were repeat spawners, 12 percent in the 1955 run, and 3 percent in the 1956 run.[6]

How do the fishes, who seem to be masters of global oceanic navigation without man's sophisticated electronic equipment, get around the world? Izaak Walton in *The Compleat Angler,* published in 1653, was the first writer to mention the "marking" of salmon with a ribbon tied to their tails, to learn if they actually returned to their natal river, for the belief was prevalent in his time that the smolts were a different species than the fish that came up from the sea. Many salmon, in fact, return as grilse or "jacks" after spending only one winter in the ocean; they are much smaller than those who spend two, three, or four years, so the confusion was understandable in an unscientific age.

Speculation on the means whereby salmonids manage their extensive oceanic jaunts must take into consideration the following facts, according to Dr. Ferris Neave in a paper, "Ocean Migrations of Pacific Salmon," published in 1964 by the Canadian Fisheries Research Board: "(a) Salmon can reach preferred distant feeding areas and can return to precise coastal localities without relying on transportation by currents. (b) Salmon 'starting' from a common point on the high seas [as around Adak in the Aleutians] can maintain widely divergent courses over long distances toward their respective widely separated places of origin [such as the Columbia River drainage]. (c) Salmon from widely separated high-seas localities can converge on a coastal locality, arriving at the latter with a high degree of precision in timing." These feats, according to Neave, can be explained on the basis that the fishes have an "internal clock" or, as he puts it, a "diurnal rhythmic sense" which allows them to make the proper adjustments to the lengthening or shortening of the days and the changing of the seasons.[7]

In a paper entitled *Models of Oceanic Migrations of Pacific Salmon and Comments on Guidance Mechanisms,* Dr. William F. Royce, Dr. Lynwood Smith, and Alan C. Hartt argue that the fishes cover their predestined orbits with the help of minute electrical voltages in the water to which they are attuned, and they also follow the currents but swim ahead of them.[8] The migration, says the biologist Leon Verhoeven, "is not direct; it involves crossing from one ocean current to another and frequent adjustments (due to overshooting) of the course occur."[9] How many of the millions of salmon cruising around the north Pacific crisscross each other's paths, zigzag up and down the long routes, we do not know, but that the great bulk eventually go back to their own rivers—even when Asiatic and North American fishes are swimming together —is no longer an interesting hypothesis but a fact.

Numerous theories have been offered to solve the mystery of their navigation. But since each has weaknesses, we are led to conclude, at this stage of our knowledge, that as one expert on bird migration says, "The ability is so extraordinary that the solution of the problem can hardly fail to be extraordinary in itself."

We are on firmer ground in explaining how the salmon find the outlet of their home river after wandering around for months and years in the sunless north Pacific, where the cloud cover is 70 to 80 percent in summer and much more in winter, and the moon and stars are usually veiled by clouds. A salmon, according to one theory, "is practically forced to return to fresh water by the buoyancy of the fat which he stores up," says Brian Curtis in his *Life Story of the Fish*. "He comes down from the river a thin little fish, well adapted to the heavier salt water he is about to enter. For a year or two his food goes into growth [a chinook, for example, may attain a weight of a hundred pounds or more]. Then, in the last year before he matures, he starts to put on fat, and he eventually becomes so buoyant that he seeks the less dense fresh water in order to be able to handle himself with more comfort."[10]

Ascent of the River

That the salmon usually return to their home stream, no matter how far it may be from the ocean or how obscure, is no longer disputed. Innumerable young fishes were marked before they left home, recaptured in the ocean, then released and captured again in their natal waters by anglers or netsmen who recognized the markings and sent the specimens to the agencies conducting the studies. There have been so many such recaptures that the law of probability indicates that the return to the home stream is part of the life cycle. Moreover, other experiments in Europe and North America substantiate the belief that salmon, like homing pigeons,

cannot be misled into returning to an alien stream. Thus kelts
(spawned-out Atlantic salmon) were moved from a Swedish river
to a foreign stream, allowed to mend, and then headed for the
Baltic Sea where they fed. On their return they came to the river
of their birth, not the foster river. In another experiment sockeye
eggs were brought from Alaska and hatched at the Bonneville
hatchery in Oregon. The juveniles went to the ocean and on their
return as adults landed at this place. It is now common to transport
fertilized eggs from one continent to another, as from Kamchatka
to Oregon, to hatch them out and feel sure they will return from
the sea to the hatchery ponds.

When the salmon return to fresh water, they are in prime condition. They no longer feed, subsisting on the fat stored up in the
ocean. The chinook, heaviest of the species, have a greenish back
fading to silvery sides and belly; there are black spots on the back,
dorsal fin, and both lobes of the caudal fin. As they become ready
to spawn, especially the males, they acquire a blackish, muddy red
color. Sockeye have greenish-blue backs (hence are called bluebacks by fishermen) with silvery sides and belly; as they approach
the spawning stage their bodies turn red (hence they are called
reds) and heads green. Coho have metallic blue backs fading to
silvery on sides and belly, changing to a muddy reddish color
during the spawning period. The males of the salmon acquire a
hook nose preparatory to spawning. Steelhead likewise darken as
they reach the spawning stage, sometimes becoming almost black,
the males with reddish gill covers and a broad rainbow stripe
down each side.

When they move up the river, the fishes seem to know precisely
where they are headed and nothing can deflect them. They no
longer feed, although they may strike at an artificial fly or a lure,
or be caught on an angler's baited hook. Ocean life takes a heavy
toll of their numbers, mainly because they are hard-fished.
Foerster estimates that of the 18,000 young sockeye that set off
from the lakes where they were reared only 10 percent eventually
return to the river. Conditions in the river during their upstream
migration are different from those in the sea, or when they made
their descent. Now they are swimming against the current: it is the
dissolved oxygen in the water that keeps them going. Nothing will
deter them from carrying on. No waterfall, fish ladder, or pollution
block can make them turn back; many die in the attempt and do
not spawn. We may ask how the fishes identify their home stream

and ignore all the others they pass. Since a river like the Columbia or Snake, now barricaded with dams up to 100 feet and more, severely taxes their endurance, why don't they enter an alien stream to drop their eggs and shed their milt rather than continue until many perish? Instinct, and the memory of natal waters which they can identify by the olfactory sense, pushes them onward. Nature made them like that and their behavior cannot be changed, at least at this stage of their evolution. If the anadromous fishes could be removed on a large scale from one river to another so that man could build his dams and not trespass on their habitat, there would be no fish crisis in the Columbia River. At Grand Coulee Dam, which does not have fish ladders, such an expensive experiment was actually undertaken, as will be recounted in chapter 6, but the results were not entirely satisfactory.

The length of time the fish require to reach home waters varies with the distance they have to travel and the obstacles in their paths. Table 4 shows that under normal conditions it takes spring chinook about a month to get to Bonneville Dam (river mile 145) from the sea, another month to The Dalles Dam (river mile 292). Fall chinook are on a faster schedule: they are in the lower river in mid-August, move rapidly to Bonneville, take about five days normally to reach The Dalles, and ten days to get to McNary Dam. Some races that spawn in the lower river and its tributaries below Bonneville are sexually mature when they leave the sea, others are "unripe" and take months to reach that stage.

As the salmon come into coastal waters the trollers await them, while inside the river the gillnetters spread their spidery nets, usually at dusk when the light is dim. Seals and porpoises follow the salmon, taking bites of their flesh, sometimes killing them. Sea lions pursue them, but, as investigations by the U.S. Fish and Wildlife Service show, salmon are not an important food for these lumbering creatures.

In the days before there were many dams on the main stem the fishes generally moved upstream at a steady pace of about ten miles per day if they were ripe. Early in June the chinook could be seen in deep holes in the upper Columbia, but they did not deposit their spawn until August or later, when the chill of autumn was in the air. Table 4 shows that spring chinook normally spawn from late July to late September, summer chinook from mid-August to mid-November, and fall chinook from September to December.

TABLE 4

Characteristics of Spring, Summer, and Fall Runs of Columbia River Chinook Salmon

	Spring	Summer	Fall
Usual Type of Spawning Stream	Smaller tributaries and upper reaches of principal tributaries	Main stem, large and medium-size tributaries	Lower river tributaries, main stem Columbia and Snake rivers
Spawning Period	Late July to late September	Mid-August to mid-November	September to December
Average Weight (kilograms)	6.8	6.4	8.2
Normal Period of Migration			
Lower River	February through May	June through mid-August	Mid-August through October
Bonneville Dam	March 1 to May 31	June 1 to August 15	August 16 to October 1
The Dalles Dam	May 31 to June 5	June 6 to August 20	August 21 through October
McNary Dam	April 1 to June 15	June 16 to August 31	September 1 through mid-November

Source: Leonard A. Fulton, *Spawning Areas and Abundance of Chinook Salmon (Oncorhynchus tshawytscha) in the Columbia River Basin,* Special Scientific Report—Fisheries no. 571 (Washington, D.C.: U.S. Bureau of Fisheries, 1968).

When the fishes arrive at their destinations, they prepare for the supreme ordeal of their lives. Every phase of their adventurous existence has led to this climax. They begin to pair off, the female digging the redd by scooping out the gravel with her powerful tail while the male tries to establish territorial dominance. Sometimes the female joins him in driving away intruders.

Courtship now proceeds. The hook-jawed male swims back and forth in a frenzy over the female as she rests near the bottom of the redd, often touching her dorsal fin with his body, or nudging her with his snout. He may even pretend to dig. The posture of the female is closely observed by the dominant male, resulting in simultaneous release of eggs and sperm. Sperm is viable in water for only a very short time, while the eggs have a lifetime of 1.5 minutes. After fertilization the female moves slightly upstream, turns on her side, and repeats the digging in such a manner that the current will sweep the disturbed gravel over the eggs and bury them safely to a depth of four to six or more inches. Males may mate with more than one female but will drive off other males that try to trespass.[11]

The procreative capacity is quite low compared with marine species like cod, which produce millions of eggs. Indeed, the number of eggs shed by a female salmon averages much less than a thousand per pound of weight. Chinook of average size produce about 5,000 eggs, coho 3,000, chum 2,500 to 3,000, sockeye 3,500, and steelhead about 3,000 to 4,000.

After mating all the salmon die. Their carcasses drift with the current until they land in windrows on the banks or are caught on submerged obstructions. Many dead salmon can be observed below the surface of the water. In Alaska streams and elsewhere bears and other animals gorge themselves on these dead fish. As the carcasses deteriorate they provide nutrients to fertilize the waters and give sustenance in the spring to aquatic life upon which the young fish feed. Thus the new generation subsists on the remains of the old.

Many mature Pacific salmon return to the river after spending only one winter in the ocean; they are called "jacks" and are undersized. Precocious steelhead returners are known as grilse. A small proportion of the spent steelhead, like the Atlantic salmon, recover from their spawning and after lying inert for a considerable length of time, during which they do not feed, return to the sea, grow fat, make their way back to fresh water in about two years, and spawn again. Some streams in the Columbia watershed are closed to fishing at the end of February to protect spent steelhead returning to the ocean. The longevity record for a steelhead is held by a male who made his fourth spawning in the ninth year.

Steelhead weighing up to 37 pounds have been hooked by anglers in the Columbia River watershed; such a fish was reported by the Oregon Game Commission to have been caught near Corbett, downstream from Bonneville Dam.

Thus we have sketched the life history of the salmon and steelhead trout, the most valuable of all anadromous fishes in the rivers of North America. Of the hordes that return from their ocean odysseys a large proportion are taken by commercial and sport fishermen and thus have provided man with sport and food. Salmon have been hard pressed by man, especially since the Industrial Revolution and the population explosion which it generated in many countries, but even in wilderness regions like Alaska they have declined sharply in abundance.

The roll call of rivers deserted by the fishes because of man's actions is a long one: among them are the Rhine, once probably Europe's richest salmon river, the Thames, Loire (where only token populations exist), Connecticut, Penobscot, Karluk, and many others in Alaska. Now the runs in the upper Columbia—which originally had more salmon than any of them probably—have reached, in the words of Dr. John Donaldson, director of the Oregon Department of Fish and Wildlife, "a critical stage." Some of the runs are now being considered for possible inclusion in the U.S. Endangered Species list, where the Atlantic salmon was placed in the 1950s.

CHAPTER 5

Alteration of the Watershed
and Its Consequences

The habitat requirements of salmon and steelhead trout are fairly precise. The eggs deposited in the bed of the stream, under 5 to 10 inches of gravel, are protected to some extent from changes in water level, velocity, and temperature. As the fish incubate, they must be safe from predators; the temperature must not become too high and the flow must be adequate.

When the baby fish emerge from the bed and have absorbed their yolk sacs, there must be a constant and sufficient supply of nutrients in the water, starting with microscopic plankton and, as they grow, insect larvae, nymphs, and others. The number of fish a stream can support will vary considerably, as John H. Storer writes in *The Web of Life:* "Water flowing from regions of insoluble igneous rock will have very little dissolved mineral matter to offer the plankton for fertilizer, and such streams can supply little food to support fish. In other areas, rocks may offer plenty of lime or phosphates to fertilize the water, and here the streams will produce more food and more fish."[1]

Nature arranges habitats to provide animals the best chances of survival. Chum and pink salmon spawn fairly close to the ocean and move to salt water in the fry stage. Sockeye spawn only in streams that have lake systems, or are outlets for lakes, where the young are reared. If the lake is rendered uninhabitable or inaccessible, for various reasons, the sockeye populations will disappear, as most have in the Columbia River drainage. In some instances the sockeye may remain lake-bound and perpetuate themselves as dwarf-size fish (kokanee).

Survival of the juveniles depends chiefly on the condition of the watershed from which the streams draw their water supply. In fact, the entire freshwater part of the salmonids' life cycle depends on the quality and quantity of water in the streams. It starts with the eggs: if the flow becomes too low and the gravel is exposed, they may freeze or dry out; in very high water they will be washed away. After the eggs hatch out the water level must remain sufficiently high, or else they will dry out and die. Ideal temperatures are 52 to 53 degrees F. If foreign matter is introduced into the stream, like poisonous effluents or oxygen-depleting discharges from pulp and paper mills, they may quickly succumb. A river is always in flux, even when man does not tamper with it. Two of the major causes of fish kills of young salmon in the Columbia system have been the damming of the river for generation of power and the withdrawal of water for irrigation agriculture.

When the smolts (or fingerlings) make their descent to the sea, they can swim over or around waterfalls and other natural obstructions with the help of the current. On their upstream migration the adults can cope with waterfalls and other impediments by leaping over them, or climbing from ledge to ledge. When man interposes weirs, logjams, deposits of logging debris, power dams, and the like, their chances of reaching home waters are diminished. A network of dams that turns a fast-flowing river into a series of slack-water pools, broken at intervals by high dams, creates difficult passage problems for salmonids, resulting in large mortalities, and reducing the amount of spawning and rearing areas.

Streams in which the salmon live are closely tied to the land which provides the runoff. As Marston Bates says in *The Forest and the Sea,* rivers are "shaded through forests, open in meadows, gaining chemical elements from the soil of their beds and shores, receiving food from the plants and animals that fall into their currents. . . . The water of the river is the product of a thousand diverse brooks which have flowed over many kinds of rocks and soils, so that it too achieves a stability and independence of the surrounding world," but is never separate from it.[2] What happens on the land that shelters and nourishes the river profoundly affects its animal and all its biotic life. That is why, as a fishery biologist said to me, "We biologists must look to the watershed to understand what is happening to the fish." Alteration of the watershed in many ways has

done irreparable harm to the Columbia and Snake river anadromous fishery resources, as we shall see.

Effects of Land Use

The development of the agricultural and grazing resources of the
Pacific Northwest in the past century has impaired or reduced the
value of numerous streams in the 259,000-square-mile Columbia
watershed as producers of anadromous fish. The major factor has
been farm, forest, and range use which altered the regimen and
quality of waterflow in the streams. A watershed like the Columbia may be regarded as an interwoven network of numerous
subwatersheds, like a gigantic tree with an infinite number of
branches. Any profound disturbance to one or more of the subwatersheds influences the quality and quantity of the water in
which fish live and propagate. When Mount St. Helens erupted in
May 1980, millions of juvenile salmon and steelhead died in the
Cowlitz River watershed.

Under pristine conditions, as when only the Indians, who did
not practice agriculture, lived in the Pacific Northwest, the surface
of the land is like a sponge that absorbs rain and snow. Part of this
precipitation is used by surface vegetation, but much of it goes
into subsurface storage. The advent of agriculture, especially that
dependent on irrigation, initiates ecological changes which affect
the biotic community. As the land is put to the plow it begins to
contribute silt loads to streams teeming with fish, thus making
their migration more difficult, and reducing the quality of the
spawning and rearing areas. The rapid spread of irrigation agriculture in the arid parts of the Columbia Basin has diverted increasingly greater amounts of water from salmon rivers, often when it
was most needed for upstream or downstream migration. Worse
than that, large storage dams completely blocked fish migration.
With salmon plentiful, the builders of reclamation projects paid no
attention to the need for installing fish passes at the storage dams
or screens to keep young fish out of diversion ditches.

Grazing of enormous numbers of sheep, goats, and cattle led to
the steady diminution of ground cover and capacity of the soil to
absorb water, especially on the overgrazed public lands, thus impairing the regimen of streams dependent on surface water for
replenishment.

Clear-cutting of forests in the Pacific Northwest, the most common silvicultural practice, denuded extensive areas, thus depriving the streams of needed shade and bank protection. Dragging huge trees like virgin Douglas fir, hemlock, and ponderosa pine up and down steep slopes to yarding sites also inflicted severe damage to soils. Devastating forest fires like the Yacolt Burn in the state of Washington in 1902, which swept over 700,000 acres of timberland, produced similar effects by destroying ground cover and inviting erosion from heavy rains. With shade trees gone, water temperatures in summer rose above the levels fish could tolerate and ash from forest fires washed into the streams and poisoned them. On a watershed from which much of the forest cover is removed, runoff is increased in the winter and spring, and reduced in summer, thus impairing its ability to support abundant fish populations.[3]

The pulp and paper mills have also damaged the anadromous fishery, at least until tough federal and state laws curbed their license to foul the streams from which they take enormous quantities of clean water only to return it as lethal effluents.

Mining, especially sluicing river beds for gold, upset many waterways, destroying spawning and rearing areas, flushing silt and debris into the streams, and tearing up stream beds.

Effects of Irrigation Agriculture

The coming of federal reclamation projects, after passage of the Reclamation Act of 1902, in the Snake and Columbia river basins doomed a considerable proportion of the anadromous fish runs because no legal protection was provided for them. In contrast, the Federal Power Act of 1920 required the licensee of a hydroelectric project on a public waterway to take measures to protect the migratory fishes that would be affected, or make compensation by building a hatchery to replace the losses.

In his *Autobiography* President Theodore Roosevelt hailed the reclamation program as an important achievement of his administration. During his tenure twenty-eight major reclamation projects were started, including several in the Snake River basin, contemplating "the irrigation of more than three million acres and the watering of more than thirty thousand farms. Many of the dams required for this huge task are higher than any previously built anywhere in the world. They feed main-line canals over seven thousand miles in length." The benefits were substantial: "It has substituted actual home makers who have settled on the land with their families for huge, migratory bands of sheep by hired shepherds or absentee owners."[4] Roosevelt neglected to mention that some of the dams blocked the passage of salmon to their spawning grounds, while unscreened irrigation canals lured many seaward migrants to their deaths.

The Owyhee project alone called for the irrigation of over 100,000 acres lying west of the Snake River in Oregon and Idaho, drawing water from the Owyhee River stored behind Owyhee Dam 417 feet high and 833 feet long at the crest, creating a reservoir holding one million acre-feet of water. Another major project was in the lower Payette valley, and overshadowing them all was the Grand Coulee project launched in 1933 by President Franklin D. Roosevelt with the construction of Grand Coulee Dam (550 feet high and 4,173 feet long at the crest), which created a 150-mile-long reservoir backing up into British Columbia. It was then the largest dam in the world, with a generating capacity of two million kilowatts, designed eventually to supply water to 500,000 acres of land through a complex system of pumping stations, subreservoirs, and feeder canals. It was impractical to build fishways at such a mammoth structure, and young salmon probably would have perished in going over the spillway or through the turbines. Thus the salmon were locked out forever from 1,100 linear miles of the river above the dam.

In 1947 the Bureau of Reclamation published its *Comprehensive Report on the Development of the Water Resources of the Columbia River* for review prior to submission to the Congress. Seemingly the bureau had surveyed every stream in the United States portion of the watershed where irrigation projects could be built, and benefits would exceed costs, the irrigated areas to be partly subsidized by revenues from power generated at the dams. In fact, Secretary of the Interior Julius Krug claimed that the costs of the total program outlined in the report "would be exceeded by potential revenues of more than $560 million." Nothing was said, however, about the value of immense potential losses of anadromous fish if these projects were built.

The program envisioned bringing water to 3,840,000 acres of new land and supplemental irrigation to 1,520,000 acres of land already in farms, encompassing 50,000 to 70,000 new farming opportunities. There would also be new industries using large blocks of power, rural electrification, and low-cost power for urban homes, factories, and shops. Inland water navigation would be expanded, and the menace of heavy destruction from floods would be removed.

The report revealed that by 1947 there had been a considerable loss of salmon and steelhead habitat in the Columbia-Snake drainage. Thus, salmon used to go up the Snake to Shoshone Falls, where Lewis and Clark had smoked pipes of peace with Indian chiefs, the interpreter Sacajawea at their side, until a private utility company built a dam without a fishway at Swan Falls in 1910. Although later a fishway was provided around the dam, "there is little evidence that salmon or steelhead now use the main Snake and its tributaries" in that part of the basin. Thus began the relentless process of chopping off the Snake River and some of its tributaries piece by piece, preventing the passage of anadromous fishes to their spawning grounds.

Arrowrock and Owyhee storage dams had locked out the salmon in the upper waters of the Boise and Owyhee rivers, respectively, "while the lower courses of these streams have been ruined for spawning purposes because of siltation or reduced flows." Some steelhead, however, were still reported in the lower Owyhee. Black Canyon Dam, 40 miles above the mouth of the Payette River, barred the fishes from the upper waters of that river. Chinook came up to the foot of the dam for several years but eventually disappeared, "possibly because of excessively high temperatures." Some hardy fall chinook were believed to be still coming to spawn in the excellent riffles of the lower Payette. The Malheur River salmon met a similar fate: "storage and diversion dams isolated the most productive spawning areas," while siltation, low flows, and high temperatures in the unobstructed stretches made them of little value as anadromous fish habitat.

Fortunately, the Salmon River and its tributaries, which contributed a large portion of the Snake River runs, were still in good condition in 1947, famous for their spring, summer, and fall chinook and the bluebacks that migrated to the lakes in Stanley basin in the upper drainage area. Not so fortunate were the upper parts of the Powder River, blockaded by dams, and the upper Grande Ronde, temporarily rendered unsuitable for salmon by mining operations. Blueback no longer came up to beautiful Wallowa Lake. However, on the whole the Grande Ronde, Imnaha, and Powder rivers in 1947 still contributed substantial numbers of chinook, steelhead, and "possibly silvers" to the fishery.

In the mid-Columbia most of the tributaries were still teeming with salmon in the late 1940s, before McNary, John Day, and The Dalles dams converted the free-flowing river into placid lakes. Other streams had been severely damaged as fish producers: for example, the entire flow of the Umatilla River, where early explorers saw the natives take large hauls of salmon, was diverted for irrigation part of the year; on the John Day River extensive dredging and placer mining for gold completely blocked the upper waters during periods of low flows and resulted in heavy siltation downstream. Miners seemed to be more insensitive to the needs of migratory fish than any other group of water users.

The Bureau of Reclamation report contains a map, reproduced here (see Fig. 5), showing the extensive amputation of salmon and steelhead habitat in the Columbia-Snake drainage. The report summed up the situation as follows:

> It is evident that a large part of the spawning and rearing areas originally available has been either completely eliminated or so seriously reduced as to be put in the category of streams rendered useless as the result of water utilization for [nonfish] purposes. This reduction in effective breeding area has undoubtedly been an important factor in the reduction in salmon runs. . . . The gradual encroachment on spawning areas has been in progress over many years. At first only a few areas were involved and no effect was noted in the commercial fishing. Those interested in the fisheries, of course, were aware that dams and irrigation ditches were being constructed in the higher tributaries, but the probable effect on the abundance of salmon was dimly appreciated. As the breeding areas were further reduced, the effects of encroachment began to be felt in the fishing industry.[5]

As late as 1952 the U.S. Fish and Wildlife Service reported that, although much reduced, over a third of the Columbia River salmon catch was attributed to spawning production in the Snake River basin. Since then the condition of the runs in this region has gone steadily downhill despite extensive and expensive measures designed to compensate for loss of habitat, as subsequent chapters will show.

Effects of Timber Cutting and Logging

Utilization of the extensive forests which mantle the Pacific Northwest, one of the world's richest troves of softwood lumber, has sometimes had deleterious effects on fish habitat and fish production. Little information is available on specific damage to the runs, because this area of research is still in the fledgling stage.

LEGEND

———— Migration routes.

━━━━ Present available spawning areas.

▬▬▬▬ Areas not available or not suitable, due to man-made conditions.

- - - - - Areas never available or never suitable.

Figure 5. Columbia River utilization by salmon and steelhead trout, 1947
(source: Bureau of Reclamation)

However, some reports are available, a few of which are discussed below.

In a paper, "The Impacts of Logging on Salmonid Resources in the Pacific Northwest," delivered at the annual meeting of the American Fisheries Society in Vancouver, B.C., in September 1977, C. J. Cederholm, of the Fisheries Research Institute of the University of Washington, listed logging activities with potential impact on the fisheries as (1) road construction and maintenance, (2) removal of canopies and residues, (3) spraying of herbicides and use of fertilizers, and (4) log storage and transportation. He pointed out that "the sheer magnitude of commercial timber land acreage and miles of logging roads in the Pacific Northwest illustrates the serious potential for watershed degradation." It is only in relatively recent years, however, that the federal agencies, such as the U.S. Forest Service and the Bureau of Land Management, as well as some of the large timber companies, along with the state forestry departments, have taken cognizance of the need to protect valuable fish in streams where logging, road building, spraying, and the like are potentially harmful. It is good to know, as I learned in doing research for this book, that the federal land-managing agencies now employ fishery biologists to advise them on harmonizing logging and related activities with preservation of the fish runs, and some of the large companies also have such experts on their staffs. In addition, Oregon and Washington have adopted forest practice acts to help in the protection of fish and wildlife.

The traditional history of forest use in the United States, until the conservation movement took hold, was cut-out-and-get-out logging. When an operator completed logging an area, he left a graveyard of stumps and broken trees littered with slash. On steep slopes the hillsides were gashed by the yarding of heavy logs, and erosion started with the first heavy rains, the silt moving into the nearest watercourses to smother fish eggs and fry and the organisms on which juveniles subsist. No thought was usually given to the fish in the streams by the loggers whose sole interest was to remove all the merchantable trees and sell them at a profit, usually not even leaving seed trees. There was no effective regulation of logging practices by the states in the Pacific Northwest until about the middle of the twentieth century, and little or no thought of protecting the watersheds from the mauling inflicted by the woodcutters. Oregon and Washington, the leading timber-producing states in the nation in the twentieth century, bore the brunt of this assault. Their forests have been cut at an accelerated pace in the past forty years.

No real data on what indiscriminate logging has done to the watersheds are available, but the damage certainly has been substantial in many areas. Thus a U.S. Forest Service report after the 1948 flood on the Columbia, the worst in a half-century, indicated that watersheds subjected to heavy timber cutting and grazing were basic contributors to the disaster. Water from rapid snow melt and torrential rains was unable to soak into the ground on impaired lands and, aided by debris moving down from burned mountain slopes, cascaded into the valleys. Millions of tons of soil ripped from riverbanks—some of which had been stripped by logging and overgrazing—contributed to the flood's depredations.

The Forest Service was organized in 1905 by Gifford Pinchot as a conservator and protector of the public domain forests, later called national forests. His principle of operation, borrowing the utilitarian Jeremy Bentham's phrase, was to use the land "for the greatest good of the greatest number." The Forest Service was known to follow good timber-cutting practices, and to regulate cutting on its lands on a sustained-yield basis. By the early 1960s, however, under pressure from the forest products industry, it began to depart from this policy and permitted accelerated cutting in some forests to satisfy the hunger of the overexpanded sawmills for wood. Wise use of the land, Pinchot's favorite phrase, was often ignored, and liquidation took its place, with devastating consequences for the fisheries and wildlife as well as the forests.

Instead of cutting small patches on narrow strips to permit seeding from the forest's edge, clear-cutting was allowed on immense tracts, creating in the forests scenes of devastation reminiscent of the nineteenth century. This also happened on private lands. For example, the Molalla Valley in Oregon was a pristine watershed of 32,000 acres lying in the foothills of the Cascade Mountains, drained by Thomas Creek emptying into the Willamette River. Most of the valley was owned by U.S. Plywood and the Weyerhaeuser Timber Company, and by plywood manufacturers who by 1973 had stripped the forest bare, according to Roger Mellum, the Sierra Club's Pacific Northwest representative.[6]

Dr. Robert R. Curry, a geologist at the University of Montana, in 1971 told the U.S. Senate Subcommittee on Public Lands, which was investigating forest practices in Idaho forests, that rocks and mud pouring down from logged-over areas in the Payette and

Boise national forests, estimated at five times the normal erosion rate, "wiped out the fishlife in several major rivers."[7] Logging along the South Fork of the Salmon River was the scene, according to Gary Eisler of Friends of the Earth, "of a tradeoff of practically all the values of the forest for the sake of the timber." The salmon and trout on this river were estimated by Idaho game officials as worth $100 million, while the value of the timber cut was only $14 million at the sawmills.[8]

In recent years the Forest Service's policy, dictated by the Forest Management Act of 1976 and other legislation, has turned in the direction of trying to harmonize maximum use of the forests for timber production with the need for protecting and enhancing the valuable fishery and wildlife resources. In cooperation with the state fish and wildlife agencies, the Forest Service has formulated statewide comprehensive plans for fish and wildlife on the national forests of Oregon and Washington, and other states, as discussed in chapter 9.

Effects of Pollution

As population increased in the Pacific Northwest after World War II and industrial activity expanded, thanks largely to the harnessing of the rivers for generation of low-cost electricity, water-polluting industries such as pulp and paper manufacture, petrochemicals, and electrometallurgical plants, became a feature —and fixture—of the economy. The industry which most affected the fisheries was pulp and paper manufacture, which sprang up on the Willamette and some of its tributaries and at Camas, Longview, Saint Helens, and other places on the main stem of the Columbia.

The Willamette, 185 miles long, flows northward across the state of Oregon, joining the Columbia near Portland. It is a complex river system formed by the confluence of the Coast Fork and the Middle Fork. As it flows northward it acquires the flow of many streams draining the coastal and Cascade mountains. Runoff from the forested mountains used to swell the main river before it was dammed by the Corps of Engineers, causing heavy spring floods, while in summer there was at times scarcely enough water to sail a shallow-draft boat.

The Indians made full use of the lavish salmon runs that came up to Willamette Falls at Oregon City, consisting of spring chinook and steelhead and a small number of fall chinook that managed to negotiate the turbulent rocky impediments along the left bank at a time of favorable waterflow. Dr. John McLoughlin, chief factor for the Hudson's Bay Company, built a sawmill and outpost at Oregon City in 1830. At the end of the nineteenth century there were enough salmon in the river and its tributary, the Clackamas, down stream from the falls to support commercial fishing. The situation changed with the advent of hydroelectricity.

In 1899 a tiny powerhouse was built at the falls to generate electricity which was transmitted 13 miles to light street lamps in Portland. In 1905 a small paper mill was built here using some of the power. From this beginning developed a large complex of pulp and paper mills straddling both banks, running night and day, their cacophony drowning out the music of the falls, pouring enormous quantities of wood chips, cooking liquors, and chemicals into the stream as well as noxious fumes into the air. In addition to Oregon City, pulp mills arose upstream at Newberg, Salem, Albany, Lebanon, Harrisburg, and Springfield.

To this voluminous pollution load was added the wastes of fruit canneries in Salem, a metallurgical plant in Albany, and the untreated sewage of numerous riverside communities including the metropolis of Portland. The lovely river became grossly polluted, especially in summer when at times there was not enough oxygen to support fish life. Even crawfish crawled out of the water to get some air.

The lethal effects of pollution on fishes may be understood from a study conducted by the Washington Department of Fisheries.[9] Its biologists submitted salmonids in the laboratory to the kind of polluted waters they face in streams and estuaries. When young chinook were put in a 1 to 20 solution of synthesized kraft mill waste effluent in seawater, 70 percent died after 23 days and a large portion succumbed after only 18 days: The "fish had fed well and reacted normally until shortly before death when they became sluggish and settled to the bottom" (p. 10).

In another experiment, chinook averaging about seven inches were exposed for seven days to a relatively high concentration of synthesized kraft mill effluent in a stagnant and aerated medium. The dissolved oxygen content was reduced and the pH increased in the higher concentrations: "Almost immediately after introduction of the dilutions from 1:8.5 to 1:3.1 the fish were aware of the presence of the effluent. In the 1:3.1 dilution the fish respired slowly and irregularly and were very sluggish as though partially anesthetized before loss of equilibrium occurred within 30 minutes" (pp. 10, 12). In less than 20 hours all were dead.

Juvenile pink salmon were as helpless as chinook in the presence of kraft mill poisons, the kind which poured out into the stream endlessly night and day on the Willamette River. When 190-day-old pinks were exposed to condensate, the main component of the discharges, it took only 6 minutes to kill them off in a 1 to 1 dilution, 25 minutes in a 1 to 3, 6.5 hours in a 1 to 7, and 20.5 hours in a 1 to 15 dilution (p. 17).

The biologists also endeavored to determine the tolerance levels of young salmon to sulfite waste liquor (sulfurous acid and calcium bisulfite in solution) and to by-product wastes as well as detergents, fungicides, germicides, insecticides, and organic glues (used in the numerous plywood plants in the Pacific Northwest). They also studied the effects on young fish of inorganic pollutants like ammonia and various metal compounds which are more toxic than most organic compounds. They found unmistakable evidence, despite industry denials, that "pulp mill wastes are a major source of industrial pollution. . . . Organic wastes contain carbon compounds and are generally oxidizable so that they reduce the oxygen content of water. The volume of inorganic wastes discharged in this state [Washington] is smaller than that of organic wastes, but comparable amounts are generally more toxic to fish." They concluded that "pollution has been a contributing factor to the decline of the salmon industry and has also affected the trout fishery" (p. 253).

The Refuse Act of 1899 put the control of water pollution on navigable streams in the United States into the hands of the Corps of Engineers. All river users discharging wastes were supposed to obtain a permit from the Corps. But incredibly the Corps ignored this mandate from Congress, concentrating instead on diking, damming, and straightening rivers, often to their detriment. The pollution of the nation's rivers, including the lower Willamette, continued while the Corps did nothing. Nor was the state of Oregon, like many other states, interested in curbing water—or air —pollution until the environmental movement of the 1960s forced it into action.

A state Sanitary Authority was created in Oregon in 1938, but for many years it was headed by a genial but ineffectual department store executive, had a very small staff, and was moribund.

Not until the public was awakened to the dangers of water pollution, as people swimming in Portland harbor contracted meningitis and died, did the Oregon legislature strengthen the Sanitary Authority, and pressure was put on the pulp and paper industry to reduce its discharges of sulfite effluents and to store them in reservoirs prior to barging them to the Columbia River, where the current and large volume of water diluted them. The mills were also required to recycle particulates in order to keep them out of the rivers; this proved to be a money-saving effort for them.

In 1967 the Federal Water Pollution Control Administration (now the Environmental Protection Agency) issued a report on the Willamette River that galvanized public attention and angered mill owners and their political defenders, especially U.S. Senator Mark Hatfield of Oregon. It said, "One of the most serious conditions of water occurs in the lower reaches. . . . Marked pollution also exists in two major tributaries, the South Santiam and Tualatin Rivers. In each case pollution effects on water users are severe and persistent, recurring with varying intensity each summer." Salmon can migrate in water that has dissolved oxygen concentration of at least five parts per million, but in Portland harbor the level in summer fell below three parts per million and sometimes to absolute zero.[10]

In the summer of 1967 I was invited by Governor McCall's Greenway Committee to make a trip downstream from the river's confluence with the McKenzie. We found the upper Willamette still mainly a wild river, lovely and unspoiled except for random digging for gravel by sand and gravel merchants. Its banks were lined with slender, drooping willows and clusters of cottonwood and maple. Blue and white lupines added dashes of color to the landscape. We did not see a house or a human being the first fifteen miles of our journey. Hawks, ospreys, and mergansers flew overhead; buzzards calmly watched from the banks or gravel bars as our flotilla passed; great blue herons standing in the marshes took flight as we approached. An occasional fisherman, in water up to his thighs, waved at us. Except for the marks of gravel diggers, banks torn up and piles of rubble, the upper stretches of the river were almost completely untrammeled, much as when the Hudson's Bay men were roaming its banks looking for beaver whose populations they decimated.

The first bridge we encountered was 18 miles below the McKenzie, and the first tributary, Long Tom River, 38 miles. Cliff swallows built their nests under the bridges and were swooping merrily, snatching insects in the air. Few riverside communities could be seen, for many of those that arose in the nineteenth century ceased to exist when river transportation ended. Here and there were decaying wharves where river boats used to stop, but only the ghosts of towns remained, a shack or barn, an empty, rotting store.

At Corvallis, a university town, we saw the first signs of water pollution: a sewer outfall disgorging foul wastes. The river was used to dump abandoned automobiles, tires, and other junk; a factory poured its muck into the stream despite a city ordinance forbidding this practice. Salmon were not running at that time of year, but the side channels—we were told—harbored largemouth bass, crappie, catfish, and bluegills. Remains of beaver dams were observed.

Below Corvallis water quality and rate of flow deteriorated. In places the river was so low that we were almost stranded, even though the Corps of Engineers had released water from its storage reservoirs on the upper tributaries. It did not seem possible that anadromous fishes could live in this deoxygenated river. Signs of human activity increased as we moved downstream: houses and barns, hay drying in the sun, plowed fields, an occasional village, a mill sucking its water supply from the river and putting back sickly, discolored wastes. Occasionally a log raft passed, a pleasure boat skimmed the surface with its powerful engine.

Between Salem and the purlieus of Portland, river traffic increased greatly and so did concentrations of population along the banks and evidence of pollution: fishes with bellies up, dead pigs, sludge rafts, white foam indicating the deposition of detergents, outfalls of sewers. Below Willamette Falls the river, in the words of a spokesman for the Izaak Walton League, was "a stinking, slimy mess, a menace to public health and a biological cesspool."

The lower Columbia was also affected by the unrestrained use of flowing waters as open sewers by municipalities, industries, and rural communities. Gillnetters sometimes found their nets shrouded with slime. "The normal life span of nylon gillnets in reasonably unpolluted water should be three to five years," said Kenneth Backman, spokesman for the Columbia River gillnetters in 1968, "but now the working life of such nets is only a year, and it costs $1500 to replace each one." Some fishermen went out of business because of this heavy expense.

In 1965 Congress passed the Clean Water Act designed to prevent further degradation of the nation's rivers by requiring the states to enforce good water quality standards, offering generous grants to communities for sewerage facilities. Oregon was one of the first states to adopt satisfactory standards. At the same time the Oregon Department of Environmental Quality, successor to the Sanitary Authority, adopted a tougher attitude toward polluters. In 1969 all municipalities in the lower Willamette basin, where the bulk of Oregonians live, were required to have both primary and secondary sewage treatment plants. By 1970 all but two pulp and paper mills had chemical recovery systems in operation and were keeping settleable solids out of the river. All this work had manifest beneficial effects on the fishery. The annual plague of offensive sludge rafts ceased to appear in the outskirts of Portland harbor.

Historically the basin above Willamette Falls supported natural runs of spring chinook and winter steelhead, but other anadromous fishes with few exceptions could not negotiate the falls. Cleanup of the lower river and completion of the new ladder at the falls in 1971 has enabled the fishes to migrate the year round to the upper waters, some of which, however, were dammed by the Corps of Engineers, paying compensation for fish losses by building hatcheries. Most of the spring chinook and winter steelhead that migrate above the falls are now bred in hatcheries.

By 1968 the dissolved oxygen level in the river in summer had risen to 5.2 parts per million, and that year 4,000 fall chinook were counted at the fish ladder at the falls, thanks to intensive stocking of the upper river with hatchery fingerlings in anticipation of improved water quality and better fishways. The DO count stayed above 5 parts per million in succeeding years, and the runs increased; the fall chinook averaged 30,000 per year in 1973–77 but fell to less than 18,000 in 1978. The spring chinook run, which enters the river in a period of high water, continued at relatively high levels: about 40,000 clambered over the falls in 1977 and 47,500 in 1978. The winter steelhead also made a good comeback until 1970–71, when over 26,000 went over the falls, but the number has dropped considerably since. With more favorable conditions for migration and easier passage at the falls, summer steelhead reached a record count of over 15,000 in 1978. Downstream migration has been facilitated by an agreement of the paper companies and the Oregon Fish and Wildlife Department to shut down their turbines during the spring months, March to June, when the fingerlings head for the ocean, and by the installation of acceptable fish screens at the water intakes.[11]

In September 1972 the Oregon Fish Commission announced an ambitious program to increase the salmon and steelhead stocks in the Willamette Valley through artificial propagation, restocking some streams and planting juveniles in others that never had salmonids but were regarded as capable of supporting them. While the river is much cleaner now, it is not as pure as it was in the nineteenth century, but nevertheless remains picturesque, reminiscent of lovely Welsh rivers like the Wye. In sum, the Willamette represents a unique example of success in cleaning up a major waterway and rehabilitating its fishery resource.

CHAPTER 6

The Killer Dams

On September 21, 1932, Franklin D. Roosevelt, campaigning for the presidency, declared in a speech in Portland: "We have, as all of you in this section of the country know, the vast possibilities of power development on the Columbia River. And I state, in definite and certain terms, that the next great hydroelectric development by the Federal government must be that on the Columbia River. This vast water power can be of incalculable value to this whole section of the country. It means cheap manufacturing production, economy and comfort on the farm and in the household." Roosevelt promised that not only would he develop the power potential of the Columbia river but it would be sold at low rates: "There will exist forever a national yardstick to prevent extortion against the public and to encourage the wider use of that servant of the American people—electric power." It was a telling speech and it won him many votes.

The Pacific Northwest had indeed been too long deprived of the benefits of its water resources. No river system in the United States had a greater power potential than the Columbia River flowing 1,270 miles to the sea in a stepped-down course. Of the nation's hydroelectric potential, 40 percent was said to reside in the massive flow of this river. It was time that it should be tapped so that inexpensive electricity would become available to urban dwellers paying exorbitant rates to private utilities, small towns and villages forced to generate their own power at high cost, and farmers scattered over the wide expanse of the region who were deprived of electricity because the private utilities refused to extend their lines to them.

Grand Coulee and Bonneville Dams

President Roosevelt was as good as his word. Not long after the inauguration, Secretary of the Interior Harold Ickes authorized the newly created Public Works Administration to start construction of Grand Coulee Dam by the Bureau of Reclamation. Ground was broken in December 1933 for what was to be the world's largest dam to generate power and store water to irrigate some 500,000 acres of semiarid land in eastern Washington. That same year Bonneville Dam was started on the lower Columbia, also a PWA project, by the Corps of Engineers, one of the many multipurpose dams on its drawing boards in the Pacific Northwest. It was designed to generate power and provide a navigation channel that would ultimately, when all the dams were built, link Idaho with the sea, making Lewiston an inland port.

Since it was impractical to build fishways at such a high dam as Grand Coulee, the 17,000 chinook, 8,000 bluebacks, and 3,000 steelhead trout that came that far up the river (almost 600 miles from the Pacific) were locked out of their habitat, thus eliminating a fishery worth $300,000. At the urging of the fishing industry, which objected to this potential loss, a salvage program was undertaken beginning in 1939. The fish that came up to Grand Coulee were trapped, along with others destined for tributaries below the Grand Coulee, at Rock Island Dam, 150 miles downstream.

About half the trapped fish were held in specially designed ponds, artificially spawned and the eggs incubated in three hatcheries, one of which, Leavenworth on Icicle Creek, a tributary of the Wenatchee River, was then the world's largest. The remainder of the trapped fish were transplanted to the Wenatchee, Entiat, Methow, and Okanogan rivers, where it was assumed they would spawn naturally and enhance the depleted salmon stocks of those streams. The delicate process of transplanting the adults was continued through 1943, when the traps were removed from the Rock Island fishways. Nothing like such salvage operations had ever been tried anywhere in the world. The offspring of the hatchery-spawned fish were released in the same four streams, where obstacles to migration had been removed and a number of open irrigation ditches, which are lethal to young salmon, were screened.

For a time the program was touch and go. There were serious

losses in the early years when many fish suffered traumatic and other injuries en route to the holding stations, and when diseases decimated populations of young fish at Leavenworth and other hatcheries. During July 1941, for example, nine different infectious diseases were rampant at Leavenworth with no satisfactory control measures available. In fact, salmon culture was then in the "trial and error stage, with ample evidence that many of the trials were errors," said Tom Barnaby of the U.S. Fish and Wildlife Service. About 83 percent of the bluebacks and 59 percent of the summer chinook died that year. Thereafter losses declined at the hatcheries; in 1946 they amounted to 13 percent of the blueback and 24 percent of the chinook.

The millions of young hatchery fish released into the new streams made their way to the Columbia and the distant Pacific, and were lost to sight. Now the crucial question was: would the offspring of the transplanted fish return to the waters where they had been released or would they move on to the blockaded Grand Coulee area?

In the spring of 1944 the biologists waited nervously for the first adults to return. They were not disappointed. Schools of tawny colored chinook and smaller blueback made the 450-mile journey from the ocean to Rock Island Dam successfully. They could be seen moving upstream in groups and single file. After climbing the fish ladder at the dam they disregarded the open reservoir and turned into the watercourses where they had been reared—the Wenatchee, Entiat, and Methow rivers. Here they spawned and died. A few fish were observed 150 miles upstream below the Grand Coulee Dam site. Stragglers continued to appear there until 1946, after which adult salmon and steelhead were never seen again in that area. While the noble races of fish that used to migrate above Grand Coulee are gone, the runs that exist today in the Methow, Entiat, and Wenatchee rivers are remnants mainly of the transplanted races.

The transplanted broods increased spectacularly for some years. In 1952 the blueback count at Bonneville Dam totaled 185,000 compared with 132,000 at the peak of the previous four-year cycle. The U.S. Fish and Wildlife Service concluded in a report published in 1958 that "despite several problems the relocation of the upper Columbia salmon and steelhead runs (in the years 1939–47) to areas below Grand Coulee dam was successful to a degree exceeding expectations."[1] To date, however, the full capacity of

Leavenworth hatchery has never been utilized because of an inadequate water supply. The hazards of sending young fish through a maze of dams downstream and requiring the adults to make the same journey upstream have multiplied in geometric ratio, and the result is that fewer and fewer blueback and chinook manage to reach the upper waters. In 1977 the sockeye run over McNary Dam, destined for the Wenatchee and Okanogan rivers, was 80,000 fish; in 1978, 18,000; and in 1979, 50,000.

Incredible as it may seem, the earliest design published by the Corps of Engineers for Bonneville Dam had no provision for fishways. Had this plan prevailed, the entire salmon and steelhead resource above Bonneville would have been wiped out. When the alarmed fishing industry protested to the chief of the Corps, he is alleged to have said, "We do not intend to play nursemaid to the fish!"[2] Public outcry forced the Corps to appoint a team headed by the late Harlan B. Holmes, a biologist with the Bureau of Commercial Fisheries, and Milo Bell, a fishery engineer in the state of Washington and now a consultant on fisheries for the Corps, to devise means of getting both adults and juveniles over this 65-foot-high hurdle. Nowhere in the world had such a problem been tackled. One of the key problems was luring the upstream migrants, accustomed to relatively unobstructed passage in the river, into long fish ladders. "If the entrance is not readily available," says the Canadian engineer C. H. Clay in *Design of Fishways and Other Fish Facilities*, "the migrating fish will be delayed for varying lengths of time, and in the extreme case they may never enter the fishway." At Bonneville the river was half a mile wide: "Any dam that forms a barrier imposes an entirely new stress on the fish which normally migrated upstream past the site. . . . The stress is not limited to the effects of enforced delay, but includes the effects of all the other physical changes in the environment (temperature, velocity and quantity of flow, etc.) resulting from construction of the dam."[3]

At first the Corps proposed fish passes consisting of only four conventional ladders of moderate size—like those at Willamette Falls—estimated to cost $800,000. When biologists and fishery engineers demonstrated that they would be palpably inadequate to handle the large fish traffic, an elaborate system of ladders and backup facilities consisting of traps, locks, elevators, and bypass canals was devised costing $7 million.

Faith in shepherding adults over the dam was pinned basically on the ladders: one on the Washington shore, another on Bradford Island accessible from the main channel at the spillway dam and from the south channel of the powerhouse, and a third on the Oregon shore with its entrance at the mouth of Tanner Creek. Each ladder consists of curling, stepped-up pools, 40 feet wide and 16 feet long, with a vertical drop of one foot between each pool. Powerful jets of water flowing down the ladders are regulated to induce the fish to swim rather than jump from pool to pool. Fronting the downstream face of the powerhouse is an elaborate collecting channel, with openings over the turbine discharges. Once a fish swims in, the current attracts it to the stairlike fishway and it swims or jumps until it reaches the counting board where it is ticked off by a woman inside the glass-enclosed chamber, thus providing invaluable data on the volume of traffic and number of fish belonging to each species—salmon, steelhead, sturgeon, shad, and others.

The dam also has four fish locks of which only three—on the Washington shore—can be operated. They are a combination of old-fashioned elevators with a tilted floor and shiplocks. Huge chambers, they can be raised from the river to the reservoir as fast as they are filled with water and fish. The lift is emptied at the top of the impoundment and the fish sped on their way upstream. Each lift may accommodate 30,000 fish a day. However, salmon were not readily attracted into them and they have been mostly used to lift sturgeon. At present there are no fish locks in operation at Bonneville or any other high dam on the Pacific coast.

Biologists were especially concerned about getting the tiny juveniles, 3 to 6 inches long, safely past the dam downstream. The bulk of them, if water was not being spilled, would have to go through the revolving blades of the turbines in the powerhouse. Spills occur in periods of high water, as during the spring rains or when the flow is in excess of power requirements—a matter determined by the agency responsible for the sale of electricity from all the federal dams, the Bonneville Power Administration. There was much spilling in the early years of the dam's existence because demand for power was less than the potential of the river; thus the bulk of the downstream migrants went over the spillways. Bypasses were provided, 3 to 8 feet wide, to deflect the few fish that approached the screened intakes provided for auxiliary water in the fish ladders.

The engineers and biologists who designed the fishways, and

indeed the entire fishing industry, waited anxiously for the spring run to appear in June 1938, when the dam was put into full operation. The fate of the greater part of the salmon and steelhead fishery in the Columbia River depended on the success of this novel and intricate system of ladders, locks, and traps. Many people in foreign countries, such as Scotland, where hydroelectric projects were planned on salmon rivers, also eyed the experiment. Some people had already written off the salmon who spawned above this mammoth impoundment, saying the fish ladders would not work.

In a letter to me of December 1, 1970, Milo Bell said that a matter of great concern was getting the fingerlings past the dam: "Little was known of the numbers of fish that we might be expected to handle at the dam and only limited knowledge of the downstream migration that might be expected. It was assumed that the fingerlings would go over the spillway if their migration coincided with the period of high water . . . ; otherwise they would have to pass through the turbine blades in the powerhouse. Passage through turbines was almost completely an unknown subject and we had many anxious moments. . . . Research was conducted as best as possible on certain of these items and that gave us faith that our approach would produce a satisfactory set of conditions. But if you were a gambling man you could have found some odds that the whole facility would not have been completely functional."

The cunning adults did not disappoint the designers. They readily found the collecting system, moved easily into the channels leading to the fish ladders, gradually swam or flipped themselves from pool to pool, and were shepherded into the reservoir on their way to the spawning grounds with a "God bless you!" from the designers. The unique fish passage device was a success, heralded far and wide. That year thousands of spectators flocked to watch the spectacle, thus creating a new tourist attraction in the Pacific Northwest.

Over a million fish of various species scaled the dam going upstream in 1938, of which 470,000 were salmon and steelhead; in 1939 salmonids numbered 500,000; in 1940, 740,000; in 1941, 670,000; and in 1942, 625,000. (The 40-year average, 1938–77, is 625,000.) The large returns in 1942 were particularly gratifying, because this marked the peak of the chinook and sockeye four-year cycle, indicating that an acceptable number of fingerlings that went downstream in 1938 survived to return as adults. Tagging studies by the Oregon Fish Commission in 1948 showed that the average migrant was held up at the dam only two or three days. However, in 1950 Ralph Silliman in his study, *Fluctuations in Abundance of Columbia River Chinook Salmon, 1939–1945,* concluded that "the ultimate effect on the returns is not yet clearly understood."[4] That there was sizable mortality of both adults and juveniles was acknowledged, but no convincing studies were published for many years.

The promoters of the dams, the Corps of Engineers and their numerous constituents, the Bonneville Power Administration, the aluminum and other industrial customers of BPA benefiting from low-cost power, the public power interests, the navigation interests who were promised a waterway from the sea to Lewiston, Idaho, and others vigorously pushed Congress to authorize and fund the entire network of multipurpose projects which the Corps had on its drawing boards. The slogan was widely circulated, "We can have fish and power too!" It was assumed that if salmonids could be passed successfully over one high dam, they could be passed over four, five, six, and perhaps more. The fishery interests fought back, unconvinced that such a feat could be accomplished. They tried to refute the dam builders' claims with whatever scientific data available.

Fish vs. Dams

By 1947 strong sentiment had developed in the Pacific Northwest for a moratorium on dam construction on the main stem of the Columbia and on the Snake below the Salmon River. This would give federal and state agencies time to investigate the problems of passing anadromous fish over high dams, and also to speed up rehabilitation of the lower Columbia fishery. The proposed moratorium met with stiff opposition from the power, irrigation, and navigation interests, among others.

On October 1, 1946, the U.S. Fish and Wildlife Service recommended in a "Statement of Conclusions and Predictions in Relation to the Water Development Plans for McNary Dam, The Dalles Dam, and the Lower Snake River Dams":

1. That the construction of McNary dam be indefinitely postponed.
2. That funds be made available to the Fish and Wildlife Service to carry on additional investigations dealing with the passage of

anadromous fish both upstream and downstream past dams, and for other studies associated with the fishery problems at McNary dam.

3. That immediate steps be taken to develop the fisheries of the lower Columbia River . . . as a safeguard to the fishing industry and those dependent thereon, against loss of the upstream fisheries by future construction.

4. That, if and when McNary dam is constructed, the best possible fishways that can be designed be incorporated in the structure.

The Fish and Wildlife Service had already made a study of mortality at Bonneville Dam which indicated that at least 15 percent of the downstream migrants were killed, and possibly more. So alarming was this finding that the Service was forbidden by the secretary of the interior to publish the report. However, knowledge of its findings had leaked out and was causing considerable distress in the fishing industry as well as among the proponents of dams.

Walla Walla Hearings

The fish versus dams issue came to a head at the Tenth Meeting of the Columbia Basin Inter-agency Committee, consisting of representatives of the governors of all the Columbia basin states and federal agencies involved with the fisheries, held at Walla Walla, Washington, in June 1947.[5] Two months earlier, construction had begun by the Corps of Engineers on McNary Dam.

The battle lines were clearly drawn between those who were confident that the entire Columbia above tidewater and much of the Snake could be studded with dams 100 feet high and more and converted into a series of lakes supplying low-cost electricity for homes, shops, and booming industries, and water for irrigation agriculture, without seriously harming the fish runs, and those who did not accept this assumption and attempted to refute it. The CBIAC meeting constituted a confrontation between the two camps—for the first and last time.

Arnie Suomela, master fish warden of the Oregon Fish Commission, told the meeting: "The Fish and Wildlife Service in the past few years has been conducting experiments to test the effects of Bonneville on fingerling fish. The results of these experiments have not been published as yet, but there is an indication, as we gather it, that there is a probable 15 percent loss of those downstream migrants." Also pressing for the moratorium were T. F. Sandoz, executive vice-president of the Columbia River Packers

Association, the largest salmon packing concern in Oregon; Orville Eaton, mayor of Astoria, and William McGregor, president of the port of Astoria; James H. Cellars, secretary of the Columbia River Salmon and Tuna Packers Association; Henry Niemela, of the Columbia River Fishermen's Protective Union; and many others. Sandoz declared that he was skeptical about the value of fishways: "Where we were willing to accept as protection a fishway over the dam in 1933, today we know, in the light of our experience, that it is a fallacy to say that a fishway is a protection of the fisheries. . . . Because one power dam is a good thing is no sound argument that six . . . are better." He claimed that "the Columbia River salmon fishery has suffered a $20 million loss in the last four years" and "the wealth of the sea" was being destroyed for the sake of augmenting the region's power capacity.

Mayor Eaton presented the Astoria City Council's resolution "that the salmon fishing industry should not be further sacrificed for dams that are so unneeded at this time. If the salmon runs are seriously diminished, the city might face economic difficulties. We have practically all our eggs in one basket, if you drop the basket, the lower Columbia River is going to be out of business."

Spokesmen for the fishery and cannery workers claimed that 75 percent of the spawning areas were already lost and the lower river should be shielded from additional encroachments. "Why spend the taxpayers' money for unwarranted reclamation and navigation projects before a fish program is fully guaranteed?" they asked. This is the kind of question that was asked again and again in succeeding years.

Suomela added, "When you have a series of dams on a river system and there is a delay at each dam, certainly those fish are not going to make it to their natal spawning areas and be able to reproduce their kind." Losses would be in geometric proportion. The Oregon Fish Commission recommended that "no additional main stem dams be built on the Columbia River below the confluence of the Okanogan River or on the Snake River below the confluence of the Salmon River until such time as all other possible sources of power are fully utilized."

Dr. Paul R. Needham, chief of fisheries for the Oregon Fish Commission, dismissed the possibility of transplanting the upriver runs to streams emptying into the lower Columbia. There is no evidence, he maintained, that this could be done successfully. "You can't have high dams and salmon too," he concluded.

After the commercial fishermen and biologists the next speakers were Indians concerned about their fishing rights at Celilo Falls, which would be inundated by The Dalles Dam. Clifford Meacham, representing the Warm Springs Indians, testified that "seventy percent of the Indian food consists of salmon. Without large quantities of salmon for food . . . [these] people will not survive. . . . Many other dams can be built on the Columbia River and its tributaries."

The most colorful testimony came from the aged Chief Tommy Thompson of the Wyams, who lived at Celilo. He reminded the white man, speaking through an interpreter, that his ancestors had fished at Celilo for centuries, that they had always relied on the fish as the mainstay of their diet, and that he did not want a dam at The Dalles that would condemn the fish run: "I think I don't know how I would live if you would put up a dam which will flood my fishing places . . . how I am going to make my living afterward. It is the only food I am dependent on for my livelihood, and I am here to protect that."

The lineup against the moratorium was impressive and potent. It included representatives of the chambers of commerce of Portland and Spokane, Tacoma City Light, Seattle City Light, Pacific Northwest Development Association, Inland Empire Waterways Association, leading private utilities, the BPA, and many others. Letters were introduced from members of Congress from the Pacific Northwest, who almost to a man affirmed their faith in the motto "We can have fish and power too" and were against the moratorium.

W. S. Nelson of The Dalles Chamber of Commerce expressed the prevailing sentiment: "A sound plan of water resource development is to be junked for a piecemeal method of development. It means that single-purpose dams, high in the mountains, are to be substituted for multiple purpose dams on the lower reaches of the rivers. By this plan we would have high-cost power, distant from load centers, requiring 200 miles of transmission lines, as a substitute for low-cost power in close proximity to load centers, present and prospective." Even Ira N. Gabrielson, chief of the U.S. Fish and Wildlife Service, a game biologist, joined in the chorus of condemnation of the moratorium. He put into the record a letter from Senator Warren Magnuson of Washington, saying: "In general, we can report a high degree of success in installations which have been made in the last ten years. These include the ladders at

Bonneville dam and at Rock Island dam, over both of which
. . . the spawning runs of the Columbia River pass in large part.
. . . Other ladders have worked equally well. Some of the older
ladders which were not well designed have been virtual failures.
Some of these could be relocated and made to work. . . . It may
be said that in general strongly migratory fish such as the salmons
will readily enter well-placed ladders."

Magnuson was to become the front runner in the Senate for the
Corps' program, a wily politician who during his long tenure
helped to fill the Columbia and Snake rivers with high dams. At
present he seems to be promoting Ben Franklin dam, which would
eliminate the last stretch of free-flowing water on the Columbia
above Bonneville.

The Walla Walla hearings of the CBIAC were inconclusive; the
issue was referred to the parent Federal Interagency River Basins
Committee, which unanimously concluded that it did not favor
the moratorium because "facts and evidence presently available do
not substantiate the fear that additional dams on the main stem
of the Columbia and Snake Rivers will result in major loss or
extinction of fish life on these streams." Thirty-three years later
this statement is a mockery, although of course FIRBC did not
have the overwhelming evidence now available on the impact of
"killer dams" on anadromous fishes. Yet in the June 1947 *Oregon
Business Review,* Paul Needham clearly foretold what would happen
if the Corps of Engineers, the Bureau of Reclamation, and other
agencies and utilities anxious to build dams on the main stems of
the rivers were not stopped:

> Some of the plans of the dam builders, if completed, will com-
> pletely ruin for all time some of the richest fishery resources of this
> nation. The principal streams concerned are the Sacramento in Cali-
> fornia, the Rogue in Oregon, and the Columbia with its principal
> tributaries in Washington, Oregon, and Idaho. . . .
> We . . . frequently hear the engineers complain that biologists
> cannot agree among themselves on the best ways and means of
> protecting anadromous fish runs blocked by dams. They say that we
> "hem" and we "haw" and can never agree. There is good reason for
> this. Until Grand Coulee Dam was built on the upper Columbia,
> fishery biologists had never been called upon to answer problems of
> the magnitude of those presented by Coulee. At Coulee a major
> backbone stream was completely blocked, and there was no previous
> experience upon which to formulate a plan. After the steam shovels
> had started work, somebody remembered that there were steelhead
> and chinook and sockeye salmon that would be blocked, and some-

thing ought to be done to save them if possible. The fish men of the state of Washington and the Federal government went to work, studied the problem, made field surveys, and came up with a plan they hoped might work; but they weren't sure. . . .

[The salvage] program cost something over $5 million of Uncle Sam's money. Today, some eight years after the program started, we do not know precisely the results obtained. It appears to be only partially successful; a few salmon are returning but the cost has been out of all proportion to the success. . . .

The question is frequently asked, "Why can't fish hatcheries save the runs?" Unfortunately, the engineers have been led to believe (and they still believe it) that hatcheries are the simple and easy solution. If a dam blocks a run, put in a hatchery; that's all there is to it. Unfortunately, the teachings of early-day fish culturists still form the basis of public thought on this problem. With salmon and steelhead, it is sadly in error. Even after seventy years of fish culture in this country, there is not one single major, commercial-sized run of salmon or steelhead being maintained by hatcheries alone. All hatcheries can be expected to do is to supplement natural propagation; that is all they will ever do over the broad reaches of western waters. . . .

If present plans of the dam builders go through, the rich anadromous fishery resources of the Columbia Basin are doomed. A total of some sixty-nine damsites are now under study in this basin alone. Among these is McNary Dam. . . . If this is built, it will be the beginning of the end of steelhead and salmon runs in the upper Columbia River. Another main-river dam is proposed for construction below the McNary Dam at The Dalles near Celilo Falls. But the finishing touch will be the four-dam plan now being recommended by the Army Engineer Corps for construction on the Snake River to provide slack-water navigation to Lewiston, Idaho. All western fishery biologists with whom I have talked agree that this plan, if followed, will spell the doom of salmon and steelhead migrations up the Snake River as well as up its best tributary, the Salmon River in Idaho. . . .

Commercial and sport fishing for salmon and steelhead in the Columbia River brings in around $12 million a year to Oregon and Washington. If this were capitalized at 4 per cent, the investment would be worth some $300 million. Already the Columbia River has had some 75 per cent of its upper spawning grounds cut off by dams, and these encroachments plus the losses through irrigation and power developments have brought a serious decline in the numbers of fish available. The commercial salmon pack has, within recent years, been reduced to approximately half its thirty-year average. Doubtless overfishing is one contributing factor, but more important has been the indiscriminate construction of dams, pollution, and reduction of spawning grounds in the upper areas.[6]

When we consider that Needham wrote this article in 1947, when there were only three dams on the main stem of the Columbia and none on the Snake below Swan Falls, his prophecy is phenomenal. But the people of the Pacific Northwest, lulled by the propaganda of the Corps of Engineers, Bonneville Power Administration, and other agencies with vested interests in the development of the Columbia water resources, tossed the gloomy predictions aside and the dam builders' juggernaut rolled on.

The Juggernaut Rolls On

The issue of the Snake River dams proposed by the Corps, crucial to the survival or destruction of the great runs of salmon and steelhead trout still remaining in this extensive watershed despite the severe losses under the reclamation programs of the previous forty years, came to a climax in the spring of 1952 at the hearings on the Army Civil Works bill, known in congressional circles as the "Pork Barrel Bill," held by a subcommittee of the House Appropriations Committee.[7] Into this grab-bag measure, which now dispenses billions of dollars to the Corps of Engineers each year, members of Congress toss a great variety of "pork" beneficial to their states. However, mixed with the good projects are also relatively valueless ones, such as straightening rivers (a favorite chore of the Corps) that do not need straightening; a canal that will create inland water navigation in a state that does not really need it, like Oregon and Idaho; a dam or two, like the one currently rising on the Applegate River in southern Oregon, which is a $90 million boondoggle; or one that will store water for growing crops like potatoes, sugar beets, or cotton that are in excess supply in the United States; and so on. The immediate issue at the hearing was the Corps' request for $3 million to start construction on Ice Harbor Dam, the first of a quartet deemed necessary and feasible for the Snake River, with power generation the main benefit, and extension of the 40-foot-deep navigation channel to make Lewiston, Idaho, an inland port.

General Chorpening, chief of the Corps of Engineers, assured the subcommittee that "with the experience gained in operation of Bonneville dam, there will be no difficulty at this project in the proper handling of the fish." Congressman Rabaut disagreed. "I notice," he said, holding up the latest version of the Corps' "308 Report," "that the total height of the dams on the Columbia and

Astor Column at Astoria over-
looks mouth of Columbia, and
point where Captain Gray discovered the river *(Oregon Highway
Department)*

Cargo of Columbia River canned salmon unloaded at Liverpool about 1885 (*Radio Times, Hutton Picture Library, London*)

The Indian fishery at Celilo Falls, destroyed by The Dalles Dam in 1956 *(Gladys Seufert)*

Seufert's No. 5 Fishwheel, the most successful on the Columbia
(Gladys Seufert)

The "iron chink" revolutionized salmon canning *(Oregon Historical Society)*

Fish scows on the Columbia took stupendous numbers of salmon before they were outlawed *(Oregon Historical Society)*

Above: Aerial view of fish ladder at Bradford Island, Bonneville Dam, visitors' building, and exit into reservoir, looking upstream *(Corps of Engineers)*

Right: Fish counting chamber, Bonneville Dam *(Corps of Engineers)*

Cowlitz Salmon Hatchery built as compensation for Cowlitz Dam, Washington, operated by Washington Department of Fisheries *(Washington Department of Fisheries)*

Salmon fishing in Multnomah Channel of the Willamette River *(Oregon Department of Fish and Wildlife)*

Lower Granite Dam, equipped with fish ladders, is the last passable megalith in the Snake River watershed *(Corps of Engineers)*

lower Snake is 760 feet. The highest existing fish ladder in the world today is at Bonneville, which is 65 feet and the downstream [migrant] loss is 15 percent. As we progress up this river and gain this height of 760 feet—up the Columbia and the lower Snake—we get these different elevations: The Dalles, 88 feet; John Day, 132 feet; McNary, 100 feet; Ice Harbor, 100 feet; the Lower Monumental, 93 feet; Little Goose, 100 feet; and the Lower Granite, 82 feet. . . . There must be a tiring effect upon the fish going up the river, in the vicinity of The Dalles or McNary or Ice Harbor or any of these places. . . . The fish loss is going to be something which should be determined."

General Chorpening did not accept the alleged 15 percent loss of downstream migrants at Bonneville Dam, but he recognized the magnitude of the problem of passing fish up and down so many high barriers: "We have made some progress in getting salmon over the dams . . . but there is the killing of the little fry going downstream; we have not been able to solve that [problem]."

The fishing industry, appalled at the idea of blockading the Snake River with hundred-foot dams, supported Congressman Rabaut stoutly. Their arguments were summarized by Philip W. Schneider, director of the Oregon Game Commission: "We believe that construction of Ice Harbor, at least at this time, would be a mistake. . . . We certainly do not oppose well-planned, orderly development of the Columbia River Basin, but we feel that those dams that will not endanger the fish runs should be completed before those such as Ice Harbor on the lower Snake are built."

About half of the Columbia runs, said Schneider, use the Snake River as a highway to the sea. Since Ice Harbor would be close to the mouth of the Snake, "virtually 100 percent of the Snake River fish would be affected. We sincerely feel that the construction of these lower Snake dams at this time would doom for all practical purposes a major portion of the Columbia runs." Schneider's comments, echoing the view Needham had expressed five years earlier, proved to be accurate. However, the U.S. Fish and Wildlife Service, which was supposed to protect the fishery from adverse developments, took a contrary view. Its spokesman assured the committee that plans for fish passage at Ice Harbor "will eliminate any threat of exterminating any species of salmon. . . . We believe there will be losses but . . . the fishery interests are prepared, through the best possible devices known to modern science, to keep these losses at a minimum—thus insuring that everything possible is being done to perpetuate the fishery resources in the Columbia River watershed as they may be affected by the Ice Harbor project." The author of this statement, J. L. Kask, assistant director of the Service, was a respected fishery biologist.

After listening to lengthy testimony pro and con, the subcommittee of the House Appropriations Committee decided that the Ice Harbor project should be denied construction funds.

In one of the most memorable speeches on conservation ever heard in the House of Representatives, Congressman Cannon said:

> The construction of this dam means eventually the complete extinction of a species of salmon which thereafter can never be resuscitated or recreated. Only God in His infinite power and wisdom can create a new species of animal life, and when that is once destroyed there is no power on earth that will reproduce it. We accomplish miracles in our laboratories but we have never yet been able to create in our test tubes the celestial spark of life. The total extinction of life for all time to come is something we cannot even contemplate, regardless of the need for power for the few years that will be required to develop some method of avoiding this permanent restriction of an important food supply.

The tragedy is that Cannon's words went unheeded. After the Democrats recaptured control of Congress in 1956, Senator Magnuson and Senator Wayne Morse of Oregon, determined to secure some funds for Ice Harbor, executed a parliamentary maneuver to achieve their end. Rather than wage a committee or floor fight, where they would run full tilt into opposition, they persuaded the Joint Senate-House conference committee handling the Army Civil Works bill for fiscal 1957 to add $1 million for the dam. Despite last-minute protests of the fishing industry, which was caught napping by this clever move, both houses permitted the small appropriation to stand. Thus began the accelerated downfall of the Snake River salmon and steelhead resource. With Ice Harbor in the bag, so to speak, the Corps' juggernaut proceeded in succeeding years to obliterate opposition to its remaining trio of Snake River projects.

How the Corps of Engineers Operates

It may be worthwhile at this point to examine the way the Corps of Engineers operates and why it exercises so much power—it is said to be the fourth arm of the American government—in changing our landscape and manipulating our water resources.

The name of the game, as Theodore Roosevelt called it, is pork barrel politics. While it brings immense benefits to the Pacific Northwest, and the nation, it has also wreaked havoc on many rivers, obliterated vast acreages of fertile agricultural land, uprooted incalculable numbers of people from their homes and farmsteads, destroyed habitat for fisheries and wildlife, and aggravated floods in the name of flood control.

Elizabeth Drew in an article, "Dam Outrage: The Story of the Army Corps of Engineers," published in the *Atlantic Monthly* in 1970, elucidates how the game is played.[8] A formal document issued by the Corps, known on Capitol Hill as "Eighteen Steps to Glory," lists the procedures for launching a project through the congressional mill until it emerges triumphant as a funded undertaking: then the bulldozers begin to level the site and the local congressman who sponsored the project delivers a cut and dried speech lauding its value to his district while reporters' cameras click and a television crew immortalizes the event on videotape.

It all begins when local interests who stand to gain from a project—farmers, ranchers, barge companies, industrialists seeking low-cost electricity, public power agencies, private utilities, contractors—get together, often through the medium of the local chamber of commerce, with the Corps' district engineer. He explains to them how to go about gaining congressional sponsorship, win public support, and move through the elaborate process of winning approval from the relevant congressional committees that will submit the project to the Office of Management and Budget, who will incorporate it into the omnibus civil works bill.

The local congressman or senator must first introduce the necessary legislation authorizing the Corps to study the project, and later see that it receives initial funding. In the case of the Columbia and Snake river dams the Corps completed its first "308 Report" in the 1920s when Hoover was president, and subsequently revised it from time to time. Hardly any congressman, says Miss Drew, will turn down any reasonable request from his constituents, because his reelection may depend on his ability to bring home the "pork"—some kind of public works for which the federal government (that is, the nation's taxpayers) pays the complete costs, a gift to the state. The project's promoters will form a group to lobby every year for funds.

One of the most formidable lobbyists for the Columbia-Snake river dams was the Inland Empire Waterways Association, with headquarters in Walla Walla, supported by every port and would-be port on the river from Astoria to Lewiston, the barge transportation companies, the chambers of commerce, the Bonneville Power Administration, other utilities, the aluminum companies, and others. It was well financed. Its annual meetings were held in Portland with a blaze of publicity. The executive vice-president in the 1950s, Herbert West, adept at making friends and influencing people, knew how to court allies like Paul Raver, the BPA administrator, and was a close friend of every district engineer, an honored guest when he went to Washington of the chief of the Corps himself, and a master at handling congressional committees. I knew him well. He was rightly proud of the monuments to his lifework—the sleek, magnificent concrete barriers across the rivers built in the 1950s and 1960s.

"The power to authorize the study of a project, then to initiate it, and to appropriate money for it, is held by the Senate and House Public Works Committee, and by the Public Works subcommittees of the Appropriations Committees, a total of about seventy men," says Miss Drew. They are the ones who tap the public treasury for the billions of dollars to fund the Corps' projects, which may stretch over a hundred congressional districts, providing something for everyone, in nearly fifty states. Since the number of requests that come up each year for authorization and funding greatly exceed the number which even a prodigal Congress can approve, there is a game called "mutual accommodation" that Congress plays, one man promising to vote for another's pet project, no matter how useless, irrelevant, or environmentally disastrous it may be, in return for a promise to vote for something in his district. Thus, when I asked Congressman Al Ullman in May 1979, in a letter, how he happened, as chairman of the powerful Ways and Means Committee, to vote for a $100,000 appropriation for fiscal 1979 to study once again the proposed Ben Franklin dam, which would preempt the last free-flowing stretch of the Columbia in the United States, his aide phoned me and said, "A congressman has to help his colleagues." The fact that the dam would destroy spawning grounds for 25,000 to 35,000 fall chinook, and 10,000 to 20,000 steelhead, according to the U.S. Fish and Wildlife Service, did not seem to bother the congressman, nor Senator Magnuson, sponsor of the appropriation in the Senate. Senator Magnuson later said that he was against construction of Ben Franklin dam but nevertheless obtained $400,000 for the Corps to continue its study in the next fiscal year.

After the district engineer gives a project his blessing, it moves to Washington for approval of the Army Engineers' Review Board, which is usually perfunctory, and is then slated for authorization by Congress, and after that for funding. The first hurdle is to get past the Office of Management and Budget, an arm of the White House. Before that, hearings are held by the appropriate subcommittees of both houses; here it may be held up, as Ice Harbor Dam, authorized in 1945, was held up in 1952 and "put on the back burner," as the saying goes. One defeat does not mean the project is dead, for like Ben Franklin dam it will be resubmitted again and again if necessary. "No one remembers," says Miss Drew, "that a project was ever killed on the floor of the Congress," and a parliamentary maneuver like that of Senators Magnuson and Morse on Ice Harbor Dam will get the bulldozers working on a project costing a hundred million dollars or more, for which the benefiting state has to pay nothing. (It is worth noting that the recommendation in 1978 by President Carter that civil works projects be financed by the federal government at 95 percent of the cost, with the state paying the remaining 5 percent, was summarily tossed into the wastebasket by Congress.)

There are certain requirements projects must meet to obtain congressional approval. Basic is that benefits must equal or exceed costs—for every dollar of costs one dollar or more in benefits must be expected. Often this principle is tilted by the Corps in its favor when a project is technically feasible but economically shaky. The Corps has been known to exaggerate benefits greatly, as from flood control and navigation or recreation. It will attach precise dollar values to such intangible benefits as the estimated number of people who will visit a salmon ladder or reservoir for recreation, but ignore the losses of spawning grounds, fish kills at dams, and destruction of a beautiful valley and its wildlife.

Having satisfied Congress by its weird arithmetic that benefits will exceed costs, using the low 3 percent interest for money borrowed to finance the project, it proceeds to spend whatever is necessary to get the job done, especially in a period of inflation when the federal government must pay 10 percent or more. Overruns are common. Chief Joseph Dam in Washington, for example, was estimated to cost $104 million; when completed in 1955 it cost $145 million, a 39 percent overrun.

The technical competence of the Corps, at least as builders of dams, is rarely questioned, but its promotion methods are often unpalatable. Whether all the dams the Corps cajoled Congress into financing on the Columbia and Snake rivers, with the help of local congressmen, newspapers, chambers of commerce, port authorities, and businessmen, were really needed is a moot question as the price paid in fisheries and other wildlife losses becomes astronomical. The electricity which provided the main economic rationale for the projects could have been generated at thermal plants elsewhere or on the same rivers at much less "cost." The Canadians, seeing what was happening on the Columbia, were determined to save the Fraser River, probably second to the Columbia in its wealth of salmon, and to this day have resisted the pressure of the power interests to usurp its water flow. "What they have seen on the Columbia hardened their determination to keep it untamed," the late Roderick Haig-Brown, ardent conservationist, once told me. The Corps is regarded as public enemy number one of the environment.

The Snake River Debacle

After the brief resistance by the House appropriations subcommittee against the Corps' pressure to dam the Snake River, its authorized projects moved without much hindrance through the congressional mill (see table 5). However, the Corps did not entirely succeed in realizing its fantastic dreams. As a matter of fact, both the Bureau of Reclamation and the Corps competed for hegemony on the Snake; each presented a drawerful of projects for congressional approval. Since none of the bureau's plans for damming the Snake materialized, we need not discuss them.

In 1952 the Corps of Engineers unveiled its latest version of the "308 Report," an eight-volume work which comprised a comprehensive plan, thirty years in the making, for developing the entire Columbia River watershed. If one studied the report carefully, one could see the handwriting on the wall for the upper river anadromous fisheries. The hydroelectric potential of nearly every substantial stream was assessed and every stretch of free-flowing water was to be harnessed if enough electricity could be generated and other benefits claimed to persuade Congress to authorize the project. For the immediate future the Corps proposed a network of dams—in addition to those authorized and under construction —that would impound 24 million acre-feet of water and develop 5 million kilowatts of nominal prime power at the site.

TABLE 5
COLUMBIA AND SNAKE RIVER DAMS
AFFECTING ANADROMOUS FISH

Dam	Year of Initial Service	Gross Head (feet)	Length of Reservoir (miles)
Columbia River			
Rock Island	1933	40*	21
Bonneville	1938	59	45
Grand Coulee	1941	343	151
McNary	1953	86	61
Chief Joseph	1955	175	51
The Dalles	1957	86	31
Priest Rapids	1959	84	18
Rocky Reach	1961	93	42
Wanapum	1963	80	38
Wells	1967	72	30
John Day	1968	105	76
Snake River			
Swan Falls	1910	24	8
Lower Salmon (Salmon Falls)	1910	59	6
Bliss	1949	70	5
Brownlee	1958	272	57
Oxbow	1961	122	12
Ice Harbor	1961	97	32
Hells Canyon	1967	213	22
Lower Monumental	1969	100	29
Little Goose	1970	100	37
Lower Granite	1973	100	39

SOURCE: *Columbia River Fish Runs and Fisheries, 1957–1977* (Oregon Fish and Wildlife Commission and Washington Department of Fisheries), vol. 2, no. 3 (December 1978).

*Original head was 51 feet before Wanapum was built.

The Corps of Engineers assured Congress that "almost complete control of runoff" could be accomplished if this plan was carried out, and flood damages would be almost entirely eliminated. Some of the dams proposed boggled the minds of fishery people. They included two on the North Fork of the Clearwater, 367 and 543 feet high, respectively; Kooskia, on the main stem of the Clearwater, 516 feet high; and on the Snake Nez Perce, the most gigantic dam of all, 634 feet high, and Hells Canyon, 582 feet high. The ability to build these huge structures and provide the power benefits envisioned was not questioned, but it was universally accepted by biologists that each would help decimate the fish runs. The U.S. Fish and Wildlife Service warned that the projects proposed for the lower and middle Snake, "if built to the height suggested, would do serious and irreparable damage to the anadromous fish populations." At Hells Canyon, for example, "salvage or maintenance programs would be of tremendous proportions, even if feasible. . . . The fact that these dams are proposed points to the need of earnest consideration of the entire anadromous fish problem in the Snake River watershed and to the need for the earliest possible development of the lower river in the interest of fish life." From the time the new "308 Report" was released, all the fishery agencies in the Pacific Northwest were on notice that they would have to fight hard to maintain as much of the open Columbia and Snake rivers as possible, and that they must contend with federal power agencies, public utility districts, and private utilities—all desirous of taking over parts of the main rivers and some of the tributaries to generate power.

The Corps of Engineers' report was sent to Congress with the blessings of the governors of all the states in the basin. Typical was the comment of Governor Douglas McKay of Oregon, later secretary of the interior: "I wish to commend the Corps of Engineers on a very excellent report and heartily endorse the projects."[9] It is significant—and sad—that none of the governors mentioned in their eulogistic letters the warnings of the Fish and Wildlife Service, incorporated in the report. In 1953 Secretary McKay was instructed by the Eisenhower administration to cease promoting federal development of the rivers and give private and local public utilities the opportunities to build projects on the Columbia and Snake rivers. Only one of the North Clearwater dams was eventually built by the Corps—Dworshak—after the Democrats returned to the White House (see Fig. 6).

The Corps' authorized projects moved on schedule: McNary Dam was completed in 1953, Chief Joseph in 1955, The Dalles Dam in 1957, Ice Harbor Dam in 1961, Lower Monumental in 1969, Little Goose in 1970, and Lower Granite in 1973. Washington public utility districts, with their legal ability to borrow money

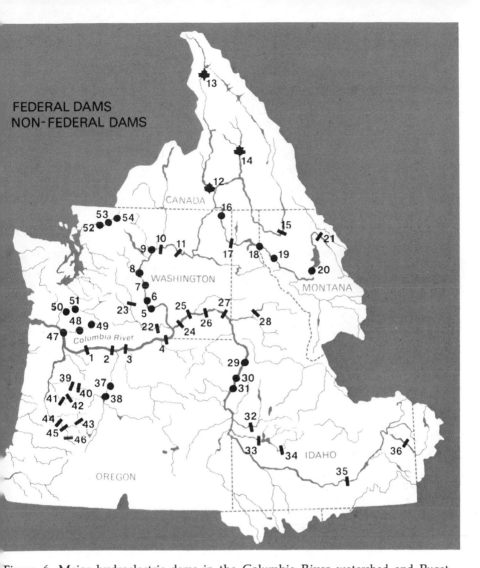

FEDERAL DAMS
NON-FEDERAL DAMS

Figure 6. Major hydroelectric dams in the Columbia River watershed and Puget Sound area: (1) Bonneville, (2) The Dalles, (3) John Day, (4) McNary, (5) Priest Rapids, (6) Wanapum, (7) Rock Island, (8) Rocky Reach, (9) Wells, (10) Chief Joseph, (11) Grand Coulee, (12) Keenleyside, (13) Mica, (14) Duncan, (15) Libby, (16) Boundary, (17) Albeni Falls, (18) Cabinet Gorge, (19) Noxon Rapids, (20) Kerr, (21) Hungry Horse, (22) Chandler, (23) Roza, (24) Ice Harbor, (25) Lower Monumental, (26) Little Goose, (27) Lower Granite, (28) Dworshak, (29) Hells Canyon, (30) Oxbow, (31) Brownlee, (32) Black Canyon, (33) Boise Diversion, (34) Anderson Ranch, (35) Minidoka, (36) Palisades, (37) Pelton, (38) Round Butte, (39) Big Cliff, (40) Detroit, (41) Foster, (42) Green Peter, (43) Cougar, (44) Dexter, (45) Lookout Point, (46) Hills Creek, (47) Merwin, (48) Yale, (49) Swift, (50) Mayfield, (51) Mossyrock, (52) Gorge, (53) Diablo, (54) Ross (source: Bonneville Power Administration)

for power projects that exceeded the total value of real property in their county, completed Rocky Reach Dam in 1961, Wanapum Dam in 1963, and Wells Dam in 1967.

The Middle Snake was turned over to the Idaho Power Company, a powerful backer of the Republican party and a strong influence in Idaho politics. Secretary of the Interior McKay refused to intervene when the company in 1953 made an application to build three power projects in the Middle Snake: Hells Canyon, Oxbow, and Brownlee. Public power interests fought the application, but it sailed through the Federal Power Commission with ease and the licenses were granted. Brownlee Dam was completed in 1958, Oxbow in 1961, and Hells Canyon, 213 feet high (compared with the proposed Corps of Engineers' 582-foot dam), in 1967. Difficult problems of fish passage faced the builders of the first project, Brownlee. The license required the provision of fishways for getting the substantial numbers of salmon and steelhead safely past this barricade. During construction about 15,000 chinook and 1,000 steelhead were trapped and trucked around the site, but at least as many went through uncounted after a coffer dam was washed away by flood waters, and many of these were lost. In fact, it was discovered that there was a larger and more valuable spawning run of salmon up the Snake above the Salmon and Imnaha rivers than had been believed. In 1952 the U.S. Fish and Wildlife Service reported that of the total Columbia River salmon catch of 28.6 million pounds attributed to spawning production, 9.3 million pounds, or about a third, came from the Snake River. According to a 1958 report of the Oregon Water Resources Board, some 175,000 salmon and steelhead spawned in the Salmon River, 46,000 in the main stem of the Snake from the Powder River to the Imnaha, 37,500 in the Brownlee reservoir area, and 22,750 in the Clearwater. About half the spawners were chinook and all but a small fraction of the rest steelhead.

Brownlee Dam was equipped with a traditional fish ladder for upstream migrants and a unique "Rube Goldberg" scheme—the term used by Herbert Lundy of the Portland *Oregonian*—called a skimmer, for collecting and transporting fingerlings around the dam. Costing $3.5 million, the skimmer was a wire-mesh net about a mile long and set some 120 feet deep in the water. It was strung on cables, the bottom cable anchored near the wings and the top cable floating on pontoons. It was assumed that the tiny migrants would not swim deep enough to go under the net. After the fish were collected, trucks would haul them some 15 miles for release into the Snake below the Oxbow Dam site. The entire complex of nets, pumps, valves and pipes, said Lundy, editorial page editor of the *Oregonian,* faced two principal hazards, "net failure and the possibility that many fish will sound and go under it."[10] And that is exactly what happened.

There was difficulty with the skimmer, which federal fishery biologists only reluctantly approved, from the start. As William Ashworth says in his book *Hells Canyon,* "young salmon prefer to migrate tail first, drifting with the current. But there is no current in a reservoir; the fish must turn about and propel itself, sapping its energy and experiencing—especially in large, deep reservoirs— a considerable amount of confusion over which direction it is to travel." At the dam, the fish had two choices, both extremely dangerous: to be swept over the spillway or down the penstock and through the lethal turbine blades. If they took the spillway route, there would be a surfeit of nitrogen in the splash pool at the base caused by improper aeration, resulting in severe embolism called gas bubble disease that was often fatal. The skimmer was designed to safeguard the juvenile fish from either hazard. Unfortunately, the huge plastic and mesh net was difficult to handle. When I visited the dam in the fall of 1959 with the Interim Committee on Natural Resources of the Oregon Legislature, of which I was executive secretary, Tom Roach, president of the Idaho Power Company, explained to us the troubles they had with the skimmer. It hung improperly from its floating boom, and numerous small holes and tears developed in it. Scuba divers sent down to repair the net at depths of 100 feet and more found it difficult to work. He asked the committee for sympathy and help "to get us out of the fish business."

Some weeks earlier Albert M. Day, director of the Oregon Fish Commission (who was with us at Brownlee), told the fisheries subcommittee of the Columbia Basin Inter-agency Committee, meeting in Spokane, Washington, that the skimmer was a disaster. The young fish were passing through the net or under it instead of being skimmed off. They were swept over the earthfill dam into the tailrace where flocks of gulls made feasts off them. "From our best estimates," said Day, "at least one million fingerlings should have passed downstream, but no more than a fourth that number can be accounted for." At Oxbow Dam, then under construction, the contractor's ineptitude or penchant for saving money caused a stretch of the river to dry up and killed thousands of adult salmon.

In the winter after our visit, one of the trapping barges at Brownlee sank, taking out an acre of net adjacent to the Oregon shore. Tom Roach and his technicians struggled for four more years with the skimmer until it was finally abandoned, and all attempts to pass fish at the Idaho Power Company dams ceased, thus creating a complete block to fish migration on the middle Snake. The huge runs of chinook and steelhead that used to pass through the wild, furious river became only a memory. Tom Roach was glad to be rid of the skimmer, I am sure, and had to build a hatchery as compensation for some—not all—of the fish lost at his trio of dams.

The private utility's mishandling of its fish problem is a major factor in the decline of the Snake River salmon and steelhead runs, which has brought them to such a pass that they are being considered for listing on the United States Endangered Species list. While the company was struggling to save the salmon in the stretch of the river it had usurped, other utilities were attempting to grab power sites on the middle Snake. Various plans were proposed, but all threatened the continued existence of the anadromous fishes in the Salmon and other rivers emptying into the Snake between Lower Granite Dam and Hells Canyon Dam. In 1964 the Federal Power Commission, after lengthy hearings, awarded a license to a combine of private utilities and public utility districts to build High Mountain Sheep dam, but four years later the U.S. Supreme Court invalidated the grant chiefly on the grounds that the project would not protect, and probably would seriously damage, the fish runs. This was one of the few high court decisions declaring that anadromous fish are more valuable, inferentially, than electricity.

In January 1968 another combine, including the rejected applicant for High Mountain Sheep dam, applied for a license to build a high dam, mainly for power production, at a new location above the Salmon River (which produces a large portion of what is left of the Snake River runs), giving the FPC the choice of two alternative schemes. Its justification was the alleged urgent need for power in the Pacific Northwest. It assured the FPC that the designs "would provide adequate protection for other uses of the water resources, including fish and wildlife, recreation and flood control and navigation." Like all previous applications for this site, it was vigorously opposed by conservationists who, in the words of Wade B. Hall, of the U.S. Forest Service, "wished to prevent the conversion of the river from a vibrant stream, with quiet pools and long stretches of swiftly flowing water, and many thrilling rapids, into a placid pond where water movement appears to be only vertical as its elevation rises and falls to reveal the ever-changing amount of reservoir bottom."[11] In 1968 an estimated 150,000 salmon and steelhead used the areas that would have been inundated by the newest proposal.

On October 22, 1970, the Federal Power Commission staff counsel recommended against issuing a license to any of the applicants, denying that the power was urgently required, since the sources of generation were available elsewhere, and affirming that the need to preserve the fish and wildlife and prevent the demise of the free-flowing river were paramount considerations.[11] However, this wise decision was overturned by the FPC examiner early in 1971, but he ruled that the twin dams should not be built before 1974. Before construction could start, however, senators from Idaho and Oregon with the support of numerous conservation groups pushed a bill through Congress making Hells Canyon a national recreation area not to be molested by dam builders.

Death at the Dams

During the 1950s and 1960s, when fourteen high dams were completed on the Columbia and Snake rivers, the outcry against them from those who cherished the fishery resources gradually diminished. One no longer met fishery biologists working for the federal government, as I did in 1953 when I began my research on the salmon, who asked, "Do we really need these dams?" One no longer heard protests in the editorial pages of the metropolitan newspapers against the piece-by-piece conversion of the rivers into slack-water pools. On the contrary, leading journalistic organs like the Portland *Oregonian* were loud advocates of water development, endorsing every statement from the Bonneville Power Administration claiming that the region was falling behind in meeting power demands, and that brownouts and perhaps even blackouts loomed on the horizon. Few people asked, "Why should we build more hydroelectric facilities when a substantial portion of the generation is now being sold to industries like aluminum and others who came here only because they can get bargain-basement rates for power?" Meanwhile the effects of dams, allied with the impact of overfishing and loss of spawning grounds through irrigation projects and land-use practices, were being felt in seriously declining runs that could not be entirely overcome by the breakthrough in salmonid culture and accelerated production of hatchery fish.

"It must be made clear," says C. H. Clay, "that the mere provision of fishways or fish-passage facilities at a dam does not insure the continued existence of their original level of abundance of the migratory fish for which the facilities were designed. The construction of a dam in a stream can have many diverse effects on the physical characteristics of the river. Water temperatures can be changed both above and below the dam. The normal pattern of seasonal flow in the river can be altered, with floods occurring later than normal or not at all. Silt may be settled out in the reservoir above the dam. All of these physical changes can greatly affect, either directly or indirectly, any fish required to pass upstream or down through the altered portion of the river."[12] In fact, even those stocks that utilize the river below a dam can be affected.

All these consequences—and more—of damming a river occurred on the Columbia and Snake. Nowhere in the world have fish been asked to cope with so many man-made obstacles to survival, and the wonder is that the depletion of their populations, though serious, is not worse. Consider the salmon who spawn in the upper Columbia watershed in the state of Washington, such as the Okanogan River. They have to negotiate ladders at nine dams in a journey of over 500 miles. At each obstacle they must find the entrances to the ladders, adjust themselves to conditions in the reservoirs (flow, temperature, predators, etc.), and have enough stamina, although they do not feed, to reach their natal waters and deposit their eggs and milt, after which they die. Their progeny, the fingerlings, must make the same journey downstream under even more perilous conditions. Fish heading for the Snake River tributaries such as the Salmon and Clearwater rivers must pass eight high dams.

"Extensive effort has been made to improve fish passage ever since Bonneville dam was built," said William E. Pitney in the *Oregon Game Commission Bulletin* of September 1970. "The U.S. Fish and Wildlife Service, Corps of Engineers, private and public utilities, and the resource management agencies of the several states have struggled with many problems. Improvements have been made, but for each gain an almost unending host of other problems has been recognized. Once it had been determined that adult fish could be passed over high dams it was quickly discovered that their young were ineffective in finding their way downstream through the many miles of slack water. This resulted largely from the water being impounded at the time of year the migrants should have been carried by the freshets to the sea. Some of those which do leave the reservoirs find only the turbine systems as outlets and are killed by the pressure changes or spinning blades."

Speaking at a seminar on fishery problems at high dams, at Oregon State University in October 1968, Lawrence Korn of the Oregon Fish Commission said, "We have presently little idea how efficiently fish pass the impoundments on the Columbia River. We know more about passage efficiency at dams on the tributaries such as the Willamette and the Deschutes Rivers. Water currents have been markedly changed in the reservoirs, or even eliminated, thus confusing juvenile salmon. . . . Reservoirs also encourage the upsurge of predators like scrap fish which feed on salmonids. Finally the water levels are determined not by needs of fish but by demand for power, irrigation water, and flood control."[13] As a consequence, "the flow may be too high at times or too warm for fish passage, or so low and polluted that the oxygen content is inadequate for fish life."

When there were only two killer dams on the Columbia (Bonneville and McNary), according to Wesley J. Ebel of the National Marine Fisheries Service, 60 to 80 percent of the juveniles survived the journey to the sea. As more dams arose the rate dropped, being worst in years of low flow (like 1977) when nearly all had to pass through the turbines and no water was being spilled. After Lower Granite Dam was completed in 1973, the full measure of all the obstructions became evident, especially in a drought year. If there is a decline in the rate of fingerling survival, obviously fewer adults will return to the rivers two or three years later. Before installation of the dams on the Snake, Ebel told the symposium on salmon and steelhead held in Vancouver, Washington, in March 1976, returns of adult chinook to their home rivers averaged 4 percent. After the dams arose, the rates dropped precipitously. Returns from the 1971 salmon smolt migration were only 2.2 percent, from the 1972 crop 0.8 percent, and the 1973 year-class 0.4 percent. Steelhead returns showed a similar trend, dropping from 5 to 6 percent through year-class 1966 to 2.5 percent for the 1969 migration, 1.0 percent for the 1972 migration, and only 0.3 percent for the 1973 migration.[14]

Since then there has been no perceptible increase in the rates of return for either salmon or steelhead to Snake River tributaries in Oregon and Idaho. So many smolts have been killed going downstream that many streams now have only token populations. Returns were so low in 1979 that, as in previous years, fishing for salmon was not permitted in Idaho, except for a few days, and some Indian tribes could barely catch enough fish for what they claimed were subsistence needs.

A reporter for the Portland *Oregonian,* surveying some of the Idaho rivers with a veteran fishing guide, wrote on July 12, 1979, "Years ago you could see 3,000 to 4,000 pairs of summer chinook in the middle fork of the Salmon River below Stanley. Now you might see a half dozen." A retired hardware dealer in Salmon, Idaho, told the reporter, "When I was a kid, the Lemhi River had so many salmon it was like Alaska. But they put a power dam in the river in the '20s, and in four years we lost the run." There has been no fishing for summer chinook in this area since 1962, and the steelhead have been so scarce that it took a veteran steelheader four days to hook one fish. There used to be nine or ten guides working this part of the Salmon River, but now there was only one.

In 1975 only 21,730 spring chinook, 7,735 summer chinook, and 16,000 summer steelhead migrated into the Snake River. In 1976 about 18,000 spring chinook were counted at the last passable dam, Lower Granite, and this permitted the opening of the sport fishery in Idaho on a limited basis. But 1977 set back some populations even further. The next year saw an increase in the chinook count at Ice Harbor, 61,000 compared with about half that number in the mid-1970s, but the steelhead count of 27,000 was half of the previous year's.[15]

Desperate situations require desperate remedies. Since about 1971 various devices and techniques have been used to safeguard juvenile passage to the sea and improve adult migration upstream. Considerable numbers of adults are lost each year between dams as their limited energy gives out and they never reach their spawning grounds; delays at each obstruction result in many dead fish floating in the reservoirs. Deflectors have been installed at some dams to reduce the volume of atmospheric gases, including nitrogen, generated by the spills, and thus lower the threat of bubble disease. As more powerhouses are built and more turbines are installed, the capacity to turn the flows into electricity is increased, and spills become less frequent. This means that more juveniles have to go through the reservoirs via the turbines in order to get to the ocean—here their chance of arriving safely into the open river below Bonneville are much less than if they went over the spillways (which, of course, are also dangerous). The power agencies determine when and where spills should take place, or not at all; in the past the needs of the fish have not often been considered.

Another device being tried to enhance juvenile survival is the installation of traveling screens in the turbine intakes at some dams to divert the fishes, mainly chinook, from the upper 15-foot layer of water into bypasses. Ebel believes that perhaps 70 to 80 percent of the young fishes can be protected from the turbines in this way.[16]

The most successful of the emergency measures taken in recent years, however, is the collection of juveniles at the time of seaward migration at Little Granite and Lower Monumental dams and hauling them by truck (called a "fish pullman"), barge, and even airplane around all the intervening dams and releasing them below Bonneville where they have unimpeded passage to the ocean (see Fig. 7). In the spring of 1979 some 4.5 million fingerlings were

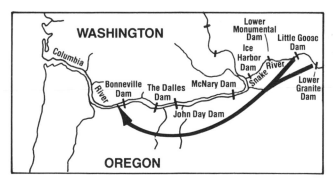

Figure 7. Transportation route for juvenile salmon and steelhead trout trucked around "killer dams" (source: Chaney, *Question of Balance*)

transported in this manner, with an unusually high survival rate. Controlled experiments show that the ratio of survival of young fish transported around the dams to those permitted to make their way through or over them in 1973 was 16:1 for chinook and 13:1 for steelhead. But according to Leon Verhoeven, former director of the Pacific Marine Fisheries Commission, "This promising measure has some imponderables. Biologists do not agree on the effect that transportation has on the homing or straying of returning adults; also, low water years such as 1977 can cause failure of the juveniles to migrate through the reservoirs to trapping sites such as Lower Granite dam."[17]

In recent years the juveniles journeying through the main-stem Columbia have benefited from the Corps of Engineers' willingness, with the consent of the Bonneville Power Administration, to release water from its storage reservoirs at the time of juveniles' migration "to sequentially spill over the dams," thus saving a large proportion of them, as Ed Chaney says in his study, *A Question of Balance: Water/Energy—Salmon and Steelhead Production in the Columbia River Basin.* [18] No special flows were provided, however, at the lower Snake dams in the terrible year 1977, and juvenile mortalities were about 90 percent.

All these emergency measures are very expensive, with the federal government bearing the greatest share of the costs. It is ironic that, forty years after the installation of the Bonneville fish ladders, regarded as a marvel of fishery engineering around the world, it is necessary to keep the millions of juveniles out of these death traps—the reservoirs—in order to save what is left of the once fabulous resource. The runs native to the rivers below Bonneville, where there are no dams to impede their rush to the Pacific, are in relatively good shape.

CHAPTER 7

The Compensation Programs

It was assumed from the very start of the dam-building program that Congress would be asked to supply funds to compensate for the loss of salmonids in the rivers. The Act of May 11, 1938, appropriated $500,000 for surveys and enhancement of the Columbia River salmon populations through artificial propagation, stream clearance, building of fishways, screening irrigation diversions, abatement of pollution, and other work to improve fish habitats. The money was used by the Bureau of Fisheries (now the Fish and Wildlife Service) to survey tributary streams in the lower Columbia watershed and formulate a program of improvements. This was the beginning of an undertaking in compensation and mitigation of fish losses at the dams which has cost several hundred million dollars. It was also an attempt to enhance the stocks of lower river salmon and steelhead as an offset for damage done to the upstream stocks.

On August 8, 1946, President Truman approved a congressional amendment to the 1938 measure which removed the limitation on subsequent appropriations and authorized the secretary of the interior to utilize the services and facilities of the fish and game agencies in Oregon, Washington, and Idaho in developing their salmon and steelhead resources. This was an important step because it permitted closer cooperation between the federal and state agencies as well as the transfer of federal funds to them for specific projects. Thus the stage was set for the most ambitious and far-ranging fishery rehabilitation scheme ever undertaken in North America and probably the world. With so many dams planned on the Columbia and Snake rivers, the losses of anadromous fish were certain to be enormous, even with the best fish-passage facilities modern technology could devise, thus making the taxpayers of the entire United States carry the burden of expenses in building and maintaining needed fishways and hatcheries, making stream improvements, launching programs of research, and the like. In 1957 the program was extended to the upper Columbia River basin.

Columbia River Development Programs

The Lower Columbia River Development Program came to Congress with endorsements from all the federal and state fishery agencies. The first appropriation under the new dispensation was $1 million for fiscal 1949, designed to maintain the runs supporting the commercial and sports fisheries at the highest possible level of abundance. No one then dreamed that in forty years it would reach present proportions. There were five facets to the program: (1) screening of water diversions and construction of fishways at waterfalls, (2) removal of stream obstructions such as boulders, waterfalls, small obsolete dams, and logjams to permit passage of fish, (3) transplantation of upriver runs blocked by dams to other streams, (4) expansion of artificial propagation of salmon and steelhead, and (5) establishment of fish refuges.

Many waterfalls, difficult for salmon to climb, were singled out in the lower Columbia drainage for early attention—on the Willamette, Clatskanie, Hood, Little North Santiam, Molalla, Sandy, and other Oregon rivers; Abernathy, Bear, Butter, and Cedar creeks; Cowlitz, Wind, Klickitat, Green, Grays, Washougal, and other rivers in Washington. Some of them are rapid, boulder-strewn mountain streams where concrete ladders have given the athletic fish a better chance to reach their spawning grounds. Scores of such fishways have been built and made possible spawning and rearing of salmon in waters hitherto difficult for migratory fish or totally inaccessible.

Typical is the pellucid Wind River, originating in the Gifford Pinchot National Forest in the Washington Cascade Mountains above Bonneville, one of the more roistering minor tributaries where salmon and steelhead were accustomed to battle foaming rapids to reach their spawning grounds. Here a concrete ladder was installed at a cost of $360,000 that enables the spawners to glide, jump, or swim in easy stages a vertical distance of 56 feet. The ladder consists of 45 pools, 9 by 6 feet, separated by vertical slot baffles, which concentrate the foaming water to a one-foot drop, and creates an enlarged section at the upper end for separating scrap fish and counting and trapping upstream migrants. Ample runoff from the steep, timbered mountainsides creates ideal water-flow for fish passage.

On the Klickitat River, a glacial stream issuing from Mount Adams, a series of five waterfalls were dynamited and two concrete fishways built to permit salmon to reach their natal waters in all but extreme flood stages. Smaller falls on tributaries of the Kalama, Cowlitz, and other streams in Washington have been blasted to provide easier paths for roe-heavy salmon at localities formerly passable only at flood stage. Splash dams and logjams have also been removed from many streams, thus opening up hundreds of miles of additional spawning and rearing areas.

Several hundred screens have been installed at irrigation ditches on the John Day River system and others to safeguard the passage of young fishes. At one screen on the main stem of the Salmon River in Idaho, for example, 15,000 young salmon were counted in a 30-day period. The Lemhi River in Idaho had only a meager stock of salmon before 85 irrigation diversions were screened in the 1950s. By 1961 the run had increased to over 4,000 fish.

Breakthrough in Salmon Culture

The major accomplishment of the development programs has been the financial and technical aid given to artificial propagation of salmon and steelhead, thus stimulating a breakthrough in the art of salmon culture.

The first Pacific salmon hatchery was built by the U.S. Fish Commission on the McCloud River in northern California in 1872. The first salmon hatchery in the Columbia River basin was constructed in 1877 on the Clackamas River in Oregon. Several additional large stations were built around the turn of the century in the false belief that nothing more was needed to restore dwindling stocks than to plant the streams each year with millions of artificially bred fry and send them off to sea. The station at Ontario, Oregon, on the Snake, for example, had a capacity of incubating 65 million eggs, and the central hatchery at Bonneville had a 60-million egg capacity. By 1900 Washington alone had 14 salmon hatcheries with the capacity to produce 58 million fry. Fish culturists assumed in those "dark ages" that more adult fish could be produced from a given supply of eggs than in the wild.

These assumptions and aspirations naturally failed to material-
ize, mainly because little was known of the biology, diseases,
dietary needs, feeding, and rearing of young salmon and steelhead,
and especially about their ability to survive in the ocean. One of
the first steps in clearing away ignorance about salmon culture was
to develop scientific knowledge about the food requirements of
the fish. Growth and survival depend on two factors—water and
diet. Water temperature is a controlling factor in the rearing of
young fish, but its mineral content also affects survival. Research-
ers at the Western Fish Nutrition Laboratory built by the U.S. Fish
and Wildlife Service in 1950 on the Little White Salmon River
near Cook, Washington, under the Columbia River Development
Program, found that they must have certain minerals in their
water. This discovery took much of the guesswork out of the
location of hatcheries and made it possible to improve the output
of existing hatcheries through the addition of minerals lacking in
water supplies.

For the first time, studies of fish diets were directed specifically
to salmon propagation. Since these fishes have a rudimentary pan-
creas and low production of insulin, they cannot be fed food high
in carbohydrates and require expensive protein. As more hatcheries were built, the food item not only became more costly but at
times an adequate supply was hard to obtain, since it consisted
mostly of packing house and cannery scrap. With the help of the
Western Fish Nutrition Laboratory findings, Oregon State University food scientists and Oregon Fish Commission biologists developed the Oregon pellet which revolutionized salmon culture
throughout the world.

The early hatcheries were characterized by large egg takes and
early releases of the fry, keeping feeding costs to a minimum.
Almost nothing was known about their viability in the sea. It was
therefore not astonishing that only a tiny proportion of the millions of fish released each year reached adulthood and returned to
the hatcheries. In fact, there were relatively few data on the rates
of returns or total survivals. The fish were victims of improper
diets and feeding techniques, inadequate disease control in the
hatcheries, and general ignorance of release timing. As knowledge
of these matters accumulated, the practice of releasing coho, chinook, and steelhead in the fry stage gave way to the rearing of
older and larger fish before sending them off to the ocean. Thus
coho smolts in the Columbia River, propagated in hatcheries as in

the wild, are usually yearlings, while fall chinook are kept 30 to 120 days before release, and steelhead about one year if they attain the size of wild smolts (4 to 8 inches) and longer if necessary.

If you visited a salmon hatchery anywhere in the United States in the early 1950s, like the one at Bonneville built early in the century, you saw a butcher shop on the premises. The diet fed the fish consisted of ground-up fish fillet scrap, rockfish carcasses, salmon and tuna viscera, the heads, eyes, and tails of fish, condemned pork and beef, horse meat, tripe, and hearts. "This kind of diet," says Ernest Jeffries, director of hatcheries for the Oregon Department of Fish and Wildlife, "we now know was ineffective. It was often unbalanced, much of the feed leached into the water and was lost, and decomposed food particles actually robbed the little fishes in the ponds of oxygen. Also, salmon scrap in the diet was a source of virulent diseases in hatched out fish."[1]

Salmon culture entered a new phase with the use of pellet feed. The Oregon moist pellet provides a balanced diet of food nutrients and vitamins. Salmon hatcheries in the Pacific Northwest went on a pellet diet in the 1960s and discovered that it produced healthy fish that were able to survive quite well in the ocean. Tuberculosis and other diseases that had decimated entire populations in the hatcheries became rare, although accidents and occasional disease epidemics still occur; sometimes a hatchery loses its entire stock because its water supply becomes saturated with nitrogen gas from a faulty intake at a storage reservoir.

Improvements in propagation technology have been rapid since 1960. At the Salmon Cultural Laboratory of the U.S. Fish and Wildlife Service, on Abernathy Creek in Washington, Roger E. Burrows experimented with controlled environments to breed salmon. He developed a reconditioning system that made possible a 90 percent reduction in the quantity of water needed for rearing young fish. "With this reduced water requirement," he says, "the control of water temperature and water quality and the sterilization of the supplemental water supply to eliminate fish diseases are practicable. With this type of system, efficient salmon culture is possible at any desirable location on the migration route of the fish to be propagated."[2] Burrows's system speeds up the growth of fingerlings, and since the larger fish have a much better chance of survival in the ocean, the returns of adults to the hatchery are increased, and this means more fish are available to the fishermen.[3]

A modern hatchery looks quite different from one of a generation ago. The butcher shop is gone, although there is still a cold
storage compartment where the pellet feed is kept. There are fewer
people on the premises, and the place has an antiseptic appearance.
At the $7 million Dworshak hatchery operated by the U.S. Fish
and Wildlife Service on the north fork of the Clearwater River in
Idaho, the entire operation is automated. An IBM computer regu-
lates not only the flow of water but its temperature and quality
and also the feeding operations. One does not see men scattering
the feed into the ponds by hand. Little automated carts do the job;
the computer tells them when to do it and how much to drop into
each pond. Some of the ponds use recirculated water, and experiments with warming water have made it possible to bring the
juvenile steelhead to liberation size in one year instead of two. The
hatchery has a capacity to produce 3,500,000 steelhead each year,
but in recent years there have been difficulties not only in obtain-
ing enough eggs to keep the plant at capacity but also in maintaining water quality and keeping out diseases in this type of system.
Now the hatchery is turning out stronger fish by using untreated
water, a system said to be closer to the natural environment. To
date the Dworshak hatchery, which went into operation in 1968,
has not lived up to expectations.

The city of Tacoma built two hatcheries as compensation for
erecting two impassable dams on the Cowlitz River, Mayfield and
Mossyrock: a salmon hatchery, largest in the world, costing $9.7
million, one-half mile below Mayfield, and a trout hatchery costing $3.7 million, seven miles below Mayfield. Tacoma City Light
pays for their operation by the Washington Department of Fisheries and the Washington Department of Game.

As the fish arrive at the salmon hatchery from the Pacific, they
are diverted into a collection channel and ladder leading to a
resting pool. Here they must leap over a man-made waterfall into
a rubber-padded chute where they are guided into holding tanks
and then spawned. Fish in excess of spawning capacity are taken
by tankers to Davidson Lake, the reservoir for Mossyrock Dam,
and allowed to spawn naturally. When the hatchery progeny reach
the fry stage, they are moved to outdoor ponds or raceways and
fed every twenty minutes by automatic feeders suspended from
the walls. The hatcheries have the capacity to release annually 4
million spring chinook, 10 million fall chinook, 4.6 million coho,
and 650,000 steelhead, plus sea-run cutthroat trout and rainbow

trout. It is doubtful, however, if all this artificial propagation produces the kind and quality of fish which spawned before the dams were built—at least in the opinion of anglers.

The Federal Power Commission in granting a license to the city of Tacoma for the controversial dams concluded that they were needed for the production of power in the Seattle-Tacoma area, dominated by the Boeing Airplane Company, and for flood control and other benefits, and asserted that "a fishery protection program can be evolved which will prevent undue loss of fishery values in relation to other values." As in other cases where a first-rate salmon and steelhead stream was sacrificed to the demand for electricity which could have been generated from thermal sources, it is difficult to tell if the compensation was adequate. Certainly sportsmen do not think so.

The Mayfield and Mossyrock dams were built in defiance of a Washington state law barring such structures over 25 feet high on tributaries of the Columbia below McNary Dam except the north fork of the Lewis and the Big White Salmon rivers, each of which already had high dams. Oregon passed similar legislation covering the Lewis and Clark, Clatskanie, Scappoose, and other lower Columbia streams. The state of Washington appealed the FPC license to the city of Tacoma all the way to the U.S. Supreme Court and lost. Thus the state gained two power plants with the combined kilowatt capacity equal to Bonneville Dam and two mammoth hatcheries.

Similarly, the state of Oregon fought the efforts of the Portland General Electric Company to take over the upper Deschutes River, one of the nation's best trout streams, by building Pelton and Round Butte dams. The issue, as in the Cowlitz case, was whether a state has the right to control a river flowing entirely within its boundaries. The state, supported by conservation organizations, such as the National Wildlife Federation and Izaak Walton League, lost the case, which also went all the way to the U.S. Supreme Court. It gained two dams which deface the scenic upper Deschutes River flowing through a gray-brown desert landscape, and which have curtailed the salmon and steelhead runs. The fish-passage facility at Pelton, with a skimmer to get the juvenile salmonids downstream and into the Columbia, failed, and thus the fish were locked out forever from the upper part of the watershed. Portland General Electric Company made compensation with a hatchery which, according to anglers, produces fish that are no match in gaminess for the wild salmon they used to catch in the Deschutes. The Pelton controversy left bitter memories among Oregonians who fought to keep their salmon and steelhead rivers unblockaded.

Results of Hatchery Operations

Considerable efforts have been made to evaluate the impact of the stupendous artificial propagation program on the salmon and steelhead runs. The National Marine Fisheries Service reported in 1970 that between 1964 and 1968 about 35 percent of the fall chinook taken by commercial gear offshore and in the river below Bonneville, and some 50 percent of those caught above Bonneville, were of hatchery origin. The Oregon Fish and Wildlife Department estimated that over half the coho landed in the troll fishery off the Oregon Coast in 1969 were artificially produced. The Washington Department of Fisheries reported similar findings. The coho run in the Columbia almost reached the vanishing point by 1959 when only 120,000 pounds were landed in the commercial fishery, compared with 6 to 7 million pounds in the 1920s (see Appendix Table 1). However, the release of millions of coho from the hatcheries, owing to the breakthrough in salmon culture, enabled this species to make a sensational comeback, at least temporarily, in the Columbia River. Twenty-one hatcheries were built by 1975 under the Fishery Development Program, and additional ones by state agencies, private utilities, public utility districts, and the Corps of Engineers.

The main products of these plants are fall chinook, coho, and steelhead. The increasing success in breeding winter steelhead helped to sustain its runs. Only recently has it been possible to breed summer steelhead with reasonable success. However, in the late 1970s steelhead runs above Bonneville began to decrease sharply, owing to heavy juvenile mortalities at the dams. This resulted in a steady drop in adult returns to their home streams. As would be expected, the rates of return are proportionate to the obstacles they must overcome in the river.

However, hatchery stocks did rebuilt some depleted runs in Oregon and Washington below Bonneville. For example, the Skamania steelhead hatchery on the west fork of the Washougal River sustains an annual run of 25,000 in twenty major rivers.

Fred Cleaver of the National Marine Fisheries Service reported at the 1976 symposium that in the fiscal year 1974 some forty hatcheries released 155 million juvenile salmon and steelhead in the Columbia basin, a fivefold increase over 1960. The greatest number were coho, followed by spring chinook, fall chinook, and steelhead. Cleaver estimated that the hatcheries responsible for this production represented an investment of $180 million, the great bulk of it by the federal government. Annual operating expenses were $6.5 million, of which Oregon and Washington accounted for $500,000, public utilities $1.2 million, and federal agencies (Corps of Engineers, U.S. Fish and Wildlife Service, and National Marine Fisheries Service) the remaining $4.8 million. The releases were expected to add annually 2 million coho and 1 million chinook to the fisheries. Sportsmen alone were expected to take 750,000 of these fish, mainly in saltwater. He concluded that "the several fishery agencies have made good progress toward the objectives that have been established in the past. Losses [of wild fish] have been replaced to a surprising degree, entirely new runs have been started in barren drainages [such as the Willamette above the falls], and vigorous fisheries are still being established. The fishery agencies are gradually developing better methods of producing fish in hatcheries. Recent technical progress has not been as explosive as it perhaps was 10 or 15 years ago, but it has certainly been encouraging."[4]

Is Compensation Adequate?

In the years since Cleaver made his report there has been a diminution in steelhead, coho, and fall chinook upriver runs, owing to the difficulties of passage both upstream and downstream. Thus questions are being raised about the artificial breeding program, where it is going, and what hope remains about its ability to compensate fully for continued losses of habitat and mortality at the dams. With the construction of additional powerhouses at Bonneville, McNary, and other dams, in response to the insatiable demand for power, there is less waterflow for the fishes in the reservoirs at times of need. Fishes have a low priority in relation to power and irrigation needs.

A memorandum circulated within the U.S. Fish and Wildlife Service in early 1979—according to a reporter in the Portland *Oregonian* of July 10, 1979—"sharply questioned making major expansions of Northwest hatcheries in general without additional research. [It] pointed to increased hatchery releases of coho and chinook without getting significant gains in adult returns. Fred Vincent, assistant regional director for fisheries, acknowledged . . . that the service has strong concerns that releasing many more fish from hatcheries may not pay the dividends expected by all the feuding user groups."

One hears biologists say, especially those in federal and sometimes in state employ, "Give us more money and we will provide more fish." For example, Stephen W. Pettit, of the Idaho Department of Fish and Game, told the 1976 symposium: "Idaho's salmon and steelhead runs can seemingly approach their former levels in the future, but the role of additional compensation projects will play an important part in their restoration."[5] He proposed the construction of several additional hatcheries and associated facilities to compensate for losses at the four Corps of Engineers dams on the Snake. This proposal has since been approved by Congress and initial funding provided.

James B. Haas, of the Oregon Department of Fish and Wildlife, told the 1976 symposium, "Despite this preponderance of compensation hatcheries, we are still some distance from settling our accounts for dam-related damage to anadromous fish in Oregon, Washington, and Idaho. One can review a list of the projects which have affected anadromous fish on the Columbia River, and will rarely find a project at which replacement of lost fisheries approaches completeness. Some of the older projects have failed to provide any compensation or mitigation. This suggests an incredible backlog of unpaid debts. . . . Major sources of resource loss in this category are the Corps of Engineers' four lower Snake River dams, the Corps' four lower Columbia River dams, the five Public Utility District dams on the mid-Columbia River, and the Bureau of Reclamation's project at Grand Coulee. . . . Data exist which make it possible to estimate the magnitude of such claims, but future measures to reduce losses such as turbine-screening and collection and transportation of juveniles could significantly alter the estimated costs. However, there is every indication that although corrective measures [at the dams] are essential, and will prove effective, significant and unavoidable losses will continue. Consequently, maintenance of viable upriver runs, capable of providing a meaningful sustained yield to the fisheries, is also dependent upon the continuing replacement of such losses."[6]

By the end of 1979, progress had been made in funding some

of the new federal compensation programs, in addition to the four mentioned. Data released by the Oregon Department of Fish and Wildlife in 1979 suggest that a total of 71 million more juveniles will be released annually if all the compensation programs requested by the fishery agencies for funding by Congress are approved. These would include:

1. Lower Snake River compensation	27.0 million
2. Second McNary powerhouse compensation	10.0 million
3. Idaho Power Company compensation	3.6 million
4. Bumping Lake enlargement (Yakima River)	12.2 million
5. Mid-Columbia PUD compensation	11.8 million
6. Grand Coulee rehabilitation plan	6.0 million
7. Lower Columbia fish and wildlife compensation	(not specified)
Total	70.6 million

The total includes 30 million spring chinook, 17 million fall chinook, 5 million coho, 17 million steelhead, and 2 million sockeye (see table 6).

Doubts arise, however, about the feasibility of investing a hundred million dollars or more in schemes which, the sponsors affirm, will pump more young fish every year into the main-stem rivers where they would have to negotiate the death-dealing dams, reach the ocean and mature, and return to be subjected to the commercial and sport fisheries in the ocean and the Columbia River.

There is still considerable unused and underpopulated habitat available in the watershed, as in the vast undeveloped areas and forests of Idaho: 3,500 miles of streams with clear, constant water and undamaged spawning areas, according to Terry Holubetz, executive secretary of the Columbia River Fisheries Council. He told a Portland *Oregonian* reporter on July 10, 1979: "The 50,000 adult chinook that passed Bonneville dam this spring wouldn't overcrowd just the middle fork of the Salmon River [where] an average of 6,000 to 10,000 have returned in recent years, but it probably would be fewer than 1,000 this year." This is only one example of territory available for the hordes of fish that will come out of the hatcheries (if built), provided enough escape the fishermen to perpetuate the runs. The gnawing question is: will they be better able to negotiate the dams, even if all the modifications and schemes under way to protect the juveniles are completed? To many people conversant with the fisheries, it seems an unrealistic hope, hence a shaky investment.

TABLE 6
ANNUAL HATCHERY PRODUCTION PROGRAM (1977) FOR COLUMBIA RIVER SALMONIDS AND PROPOSED COMPENSATION PROGRAMS

Species	1977 Program		Proposed Programs		Total	
	Number	Pounds	Number	Pounds	Number	Pounds
Spring Chinook	16,833,000	691,809	29,595,000	1,973,000	46,428,000	2,664,809
Summer Chinook	1,570,000	71,070	. . .	. . .	. . .	. . .
Fall Chinook	35,806,000	402,475	17,180,000	190,900	52,986,000	593,375
Coho	10,189,000	469,527	4,695,000	313,000	14,884,000	782,527
Steelhead	9,279,000	766,732	17,164,000	2,145,500	26,443,000	2,912,232
Sockeye	. . .	. . .	2,025,000	135,000	2,025,000	135,000
Total	73,677,000	2,401,613	70,659,000	4,757,400	144,336,000	7,159,013

SOURCE: Oregon Department of Fish and Wildlife, 1979.

CHAPTER 8

The Fisheries in an Age of Scarcity

Salmon and steelhead trout stocks have suffered great losses since the completion of Bonneville Dam in 1938, the year that may be said to have ushered in the age of scarcity, and to have precipitated managerial and environmental problems which have grown in volume and complexity.

Management Problems

Management of the Columbia River fishery since 1918 has been in the hands of the Oregon Fish and Wildlife Commission, a recent amalgamation of the Oregon Fish and Game Commissions, and the Washington Department of Fisheries and Department of Game, representing the states that have concurrent jurisdiction over the waters of the Columbia and its tributaries within their boundaries. The state of Idaho has jurisdiction over the waters of the Snake River, in conjunction with the state of Oregon where the river forms the boundary between them. Under the Fishery Conservation and Management Act of 1976 the federal government has jurisdiction over the anadromous species in the ocean beyond the three-mile limit, for which the states are responsible, to 200 nautical miles. The job of the state agencies is to give all user groups opportunities to take the maximum number of fish commensurate with the need for providing an escapement that insures perpetuation and enhancement of the resources. This goal has become increasingly difficult because of the diminution of the stocks, and particularly since the federal court in 1974 under the famous Boldt decision ruled that the treaty Indians must have an opportunity to catch 50 percent of the harvestable salmon and steelhead that are presumed destined to reach "their usual and accustomed fishing places." Installation of fish counters at the ladders on the Columbia and Snake river dams has provided data on the numerical size of the different runs and timing of adult migration past the dams. With the help of sophisticated test fishing methods, tagging of migrants, and counting of spawners at the dams and redds where the eggs incubate, biologists now have the necessary information for management decisions that result in fishing regulations each year designed to provide adequate escapements to produce the next year's crop.

A report by the Oregon Department of Fish and Wildlife to the state legislature in January 1977 explains the difficulties the regulatory agencies face:

> Management of salmon and steelhead to maximize returns . . . is an extremely complex issue. Salmon produced in Oregon streams and hatcheries are caught throughout much of the northeastern Pacific Ocean. Substantial numbers are taken by both United States and Canadian fishermen from Alaska to California. . . . Facts concerning ocean distribution and area of catch must be known before comprehensive changes can be made to increase returns of fish to Oregon. A host of other variables also affect migration and survival rates.
>
> Information on ocean migration and survival is difficult to obtain, costly, requires extensive coordination among several states, the federal government, and Canada, and takes many years to obtain results.[1]

The different species and runs must be managed separately yet in a coordinated manner, as the report to the legislature explains. The various fisheries include trolling for salmon in the ocean by commercials and sportsmen, gillnetting in the Columbia River, angling by sportsmen in the ocean and the rivers, and fishing by treaty Indians above Bonneville Dam both commercial and for ceremonial purposes and sustenance (see Fig. 8). Anglers can take steelhead in the main rivers and tributaries but may not sell their catches, because it is legally a "game fish." Indians may sell their steelhead as well as their salmon.

Status of the Stocks

Fishing pressure on the different runs and the effects of the dams and other water-use projects in the Columbia basin have varied considerably, so that some runs have diminished to critical

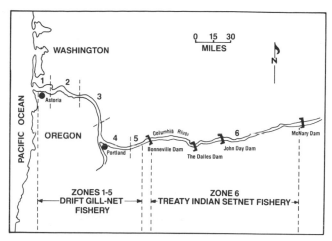

Figure 8. Main-stem Columbia River open to commercial salmon and steelhead trout fishing; non-Indian fishermen not allowed to land steelhead trout (source: Chaney, *Question of Balance*)

levels while others are being maintained with the help of enormous hatchery programs at fairly steady levels.

Appendix Table 1 shows the landings of salmon and steelhead from the Columbia River, exclusive of ocean troll catches, between 1938 and 1977. In the late 1930s they averaged about 18 million pounds annually, a substantial drop from 40 million pounds average during World War I. They stayed at or above this level in the 1940s and then, as the impact of the growing number of dams and other alterations of the environment began to be felt, dropped steadily.

The fall chinook run, though greatly diminished in recent decades, still provides the largest portion of commercial catches, thanks to hatchery production, but other chinook runs have tobogganed (see Fig. 9). According to Robert Gunsolus, chief of Columbia River investigations of the Oregon Department of Fish and Wildlife, summer chinook runs "destined entirely for waters beyond Bonneville Dam" have declined since 1957 "because of passage problems at dams and a deteriorating environment upstream."[2] No commercial fishing for summer chinook has been permitted in the river since 1964; in 1974 the run was the lowest in its history. Both summer and spring chinook runs have now reached a nadir, and

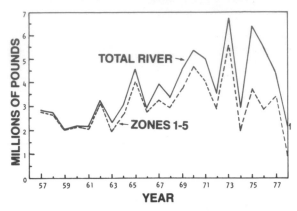

Figure 9. Commercial catch of fall chinook salmon, upper and lower
Columbia River, 1957–78 (source: Chaney, *Question of Balance*)

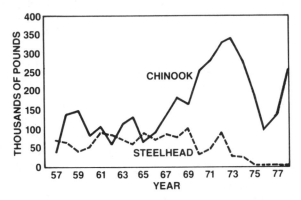

Figure 10. Commercial catch of winter steelhead trout and spring chinook
salmon below Bonneville Dam, 1957–78
(source: Chaney, *Question of Balance*)

only minimal fishing for them is permitted (see Fig. 10). Chinook
still constitute one-half or more of all the salmon caught in the
Columbia River and a substantial portion of troll salmon catches.

Coho almost vanished from the Columbia by 1960, after which
they exhibited a remarkable comeback as millions of fingerlings
(smolts) were released by the hatcheries to stock underpopulated and barren streams (see Fig. 11). In 1970 a record of over
5.7 million pounds were landed commercially, excluding troll

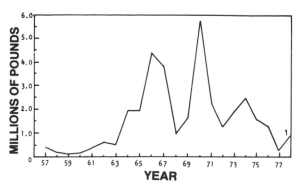

Figure 11. Commercial catch of Columbia River coho salmon, 1957–78
(source: Chaney, *Question of Balance*)

catches, but since then the runs have fallen, for reasons not altogether clear, since the hatcheries continue to breed them in large
numbers. In 1975 the commercial catch, excluding trolls, totaled
1.6 million pounds and in 1977 a mere 317,000 pounds. In 1978
and 1979, with ocean catch data available, the coho harvest, not
including sport and commercial catches landed in California, was
as follows (in pounds):

	1978	1979
Columbia River	1,095,700	1,037,000
Ocean	5,269,300	3,197,300
Total	6,365,000	4,234,300

"There are strong indications that wild stocks of silvers [coho]
are declining along the entire Pacific coast," says the *Salmon News-
letter '78* of the California Department of Fish and Game. "Some
are no doubt declining because of the usual problems of continued
urbanization, industrialization and watershed mismanagement.
Natural changes in the freshwater environment, such as increasing
or decreasing rainfall, and changing weather patterns would also
have an effect on fish populations. Some investigators believe that
certain wild stocks may also be declining as the result of overfishing. Wild fish tend to mingle with hatchery stocks, but because

there are fewer of them they cannot withstand the same amount of fishing pressure as hatchery stocks."

Chum salmon, once a major portion of the commercial harvests, with landings of 4 to 5 million pounds annually during World War II, have shown a catastrophic drop since then and there is no obvious reason for it, says Gunsolus.[3] Thus a major species of Pacific salmon, highly regarded by canners, which constitutes the mainstay of the Japanese salmon industry and is found in large numbers in Puget Sound and Alaska, seems to be virtually extinct in the Columbia River.

Sockeye, too, was an important species in the early commercial fishery; its rich red flesh has always brought premium prices from canners. In the 1890s landings ranged from 800,000 to 4.5 million pounds per year, but after the construction of Grand Coulee Dam the trend was steadily downward. Alteration of the environment since 1940 in the upper Columbia and Snake rivers, particularly loss of access to lakes where the young are reared, doomed this fishery (see Fig. 12).

One of the few bright spots in the picture is winter steelhead (see Fig. 10), which enter the Columbia from November through April and migrate to the lower tributaries. The wild stocks are supplemented with considerable numbers of hatchery fish.

Summer steelhead spawn mainly in the upper watershed, spread over Oregon, Washington, and Idaho. There were large populations until about fifteen years ago, when the full impact of the fish passage problems at the dams resulted in decreasing runs (see Fig. 13). The steelhead were once valuable to canners and commercial fishermen, contributing over 1 million to 5 million pounds annually to the harvests from 1890 to 1955. After that the runs dropped steadily and steelhead was made a game fish in both Oregon and Washington. The treaty Indians, however, may sell their catches.

Summing up his assessment of the Columbia River salmon and steelhead, Robert Gunsolus told the 1976 symposium already referred to, "Lower-river runs are generally healthy . . . while most upriver populations are experiencing serious declines."[4]

The salmon canning industry has virtually disappeared on the Columbia. Only a few plants are in operation in Oregon, of which the largest, the Bumble Bee in Astoria, now processes mostly tuna.

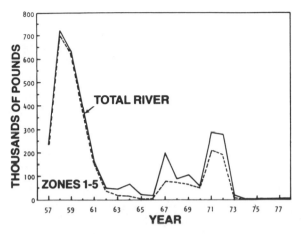

Figure 12. Main-stem Columbia River commercial catch of sockeye salmon, 1957–78 (source: Chaney, *Question of Balance*)

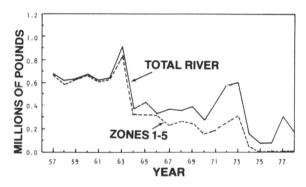

Figure 13. Main-stem Columbia River commercial catch of summer steelhead trout, 1957–78 (source: Chaney, *Question of Balance*)

The Sport Fishery

Sport fishing dates from territorial days, the white men imitating the Indian custom of sitting on a bank of a purling stream with a rod made of the branch of a tree and baited with a small fish, and sinker and lure dangling from it. Such streams now attract hordes of anglers, some of whom travel hundreds of miles with their families in campers—a home on wheels. Columbia River salmon and steelhead fishing is renowned throughout the nation, judging by the amount of attention paid to it by national outdoor magazines. Furthermore, it supports a huge industry based on the sale of gear, bait, vehicles, and other supplies. Some coastal communities partly subsist on the sport fishing industry.

Salmon is the prince of game fishes, a reputation it has held since the Middle Ages. Dame Juliana Berners, who wrote the first book on sport fishing in English in the fifteenth century *(A Treatise of Fishing with an Angle)*, says: "The salmon is a noble fish but he is cumbersome to catch. For generally he is in deep places of great rivers, and for the most part keeps to the middle of the water, so that a man cannot come at him." She tells the reader of her little book: "I charge you that you break no man's hedges in going about your sport, nor open any man's gates without shutting them again. Also, you must not use this . . . artful sport for covetousness, merely for the increasing or saving of your money, but mainly for your enjoyment and to procure the health of your body, and more especially of your soul." She urges the angler not to take too many fish at one time—the rivers in Britain were (and are) mainly privately owned and there were no bag limits—for this "could easily be the occasion of destroying your own sport and other men's also." In short, "when you have a sufficient mess you should covet no more at that time." Although written five hundred years ago, Dame Juliana's advice is as valid today as then, and lies behind the regulations on sport fishing in every country.[5]

Salmon and steelhead fishing takes the angler to rivers in the Pacific Northwest that are reminiscent of Scotland, and sometimes of England and Wales, with spectacular scenery, backdrops of jagged mountains, waters tumbling down boulder-strewn canyons that are treacherous to man and fish alike, and also to lazy, meandering streams that flow across level lands, far from the madding crowds.

More salmon are taken by sportsmen in the ocean from a boat, in calm and boisterous waters, than in the rivers, while steelhead are almost entirely caught in fresh water. On any summer morning, especially on weekends, in towns such as Ilwaco on the Washington side of the Columbia or Warrenton and Astoria on the Oregon side, there is a stir and bustle long before the sun rises in the eastern sky. Boats are tied up side by side on the slippery docks. As daylight comes, the screech of seagulls mingles with the rattle of tackle boxes, the sound of men trying to start their motors, and the buzzing of excited voices. By sunrise the entire fleet is beginning to head for the Columbia bar and soon myriads are converging on the area where the fish are known to be moving. Fishing lines are dangling from the sides or afterdecks, the boats, with their engines stopped, rising and falling with the swells. Over their radios skippers are communicating in staccato tones, telling each other where fish are being caught, and racing their boats and anglers to the spots.

Salmon are caught in the ocean or tidal waters as they return to their home rivers. Out in the ocean, where the charter-boats seek them, they are still feeding, so the angler attaches a herring or anchovy to the hook at the end of his line. Usually the sinker fastens the leader to the line. Sometimes a lure or flasher is also part of the terminal gear. When "Fish-on!" is heard, all the men in the boat become silent and taut, for the chinook may take off like a whale and keep going until the line snaps and he steals away, while the coho usually runs fast and near the surface and jumps madly in an effort to throw the hook. Although the fish fight furiously, usually the battle is short, and the end certain. If the salmon is below the minimum size, it is thrown back, generally more dead than alive.

Most of the fishing occurs seaward from Astoria bridge along the Washington side and out through the jaws between Cape Adams and Cape Disappointment, and coastwise north or south of the broad river. On a sunny July or August afternoon there may be 5,000 boats, charters and others, engaged in this sport off the Columbia bar, involving as many as 20,000 persons.

There used to be annual salmon derbies, sponsored as tourist attractions by various coastal cities in Oregon and Washington. When I first visited Astoria in 1953, I saw thousands of craft of all types, including row boats, lined up along the shore waiting for the derby to begin. There were qualifying preliminaries requiring contestants to catch a salmon of a certain weight if they wished to enter the finals, and on Derby Day finalists had to fish at a specific time, accompanied by an observer. Prize winners were determined by the size of their catches. Some of the rewards were substantial. As salmon runs began to wane, the Oregon legislature outlawed derbies, and this ban has never been lifted despite agitation of coastal communities in need of tourist business.

Almost a million anglers fished for salmon and steelhead in the rivers in 1976 and 1977 in Oregon, Washington, and Idaho (see table 7). Their coho catch was 1,720,000 in 1976 and 900,000 in

TABLE 7
SALMON AND STEELHEAD SPORT CATCHES IN
IDAHO, OREGON, AND WASHINGTON, 1976 AND 1977

Year	Idaho	Oregon	Washington	Total
1976				
Number of Anglers	4,982	272,063	706,313	983,358
Catches				
Chinook	. . .	127,490	503,877	631,367
Coho	. . .	527,229	1,195,579	1,722,808
Steelhead	2,246	118,275	89,062	209,583
1977				
Number of Anglers	29,485	304,295	619,543	953,323
Catches				
Chinook	3,682	150,995	398,494	553,171
Coho	. . .	215,943	683,108	899,051
Steelhead	12,855	145,105	100,013	257,973

SOURCE: Pacific Marine Fisheries Commission (Portland, Oregon) reports for the years 1977 and 1978.

1977, a drought year, while their chinook harvest totaled 631,000 in 1976 and 553,000 in 1977. The steelhead catch actually increased, from 210,000 to 258,000. The best steelhead rivers in the Columbia drainage in the state of Washington are the Cowlitz, Toutle, Kalama, Snake, Lewis, and Klickitat; in Oregon, the Columbia itself, Deschutes, Clackamas, Big Creek, and John Day; and in Idaho, the Snake and Clearwater and Salmon river drainages. Sportsmen now take more coho from the Columbia River in an average year than the gillnetters. They wield considerable power through their organizations such as the Izaak Walton League, Flyfishers, Northwest Steelheaders, and others. In 1964 they went so far as to put on the Oregon ballot an initiative to ban all netting for anadromous fish in the Columbia River, but it was defeated. In 1980 they plan to put another measure on the ballot making spring and summer chinook a game fish.

Intensive sport fishing for salmon and steelhead is conducted on the Willamette, where hundreds of little boats line up in spring over a stretch of 48 miles, from the falls at Oregon City all the way to Saint Helens on the Columbia, waiting for the chinook to return. In 1976, they caught 16,355 fish, all but 690 from boats, with the weeks of March 27 through April 24 providing the bulk of the catches. In 1977 the harvest dropped to about 15,000 fish.[6] There is also substantial fishing for chinook in tributaries such as the Molalla, Calapooya, Santiam, and McKenzie above the falls and Clackamas below the falls.

The fall chinook and steelhead in the Willamette are the result chiefly of extensive plantings of hatchery fish in underpopulated or barren streams. The dramatic rise in the steelhead run, from 4,600 in 1971 to 19,000 in 1978, as counted at the falls, bodes well for sportsmen.

Even the city of Portland boasts of a recreational fishery on Sauvie Island, an Indian settlement which still retains its pastoral charm. Along the sandy beach where the merchant ships from the Orient, carrying Japanese automobiles, Korean and Taiwanese textiles, and the like, pass on their way to Portland, one may see on a spring or summer day numerous anglers, mostly retired people, waiting for the salmon to bite, lunch boxes at their feet, from dawn till late afternoon. This is called Pensioners Beach. The anglers are happy if they catch a salmon or steelhead every two or three days. The clear blue sky, the breeze coming off the distant ocean, the boats coasting along with their foreign flags flying and the crews craning their necks at them, give these men and women a sense of exhilaration. Should one be lucky enough to take home a gleaming ten or twelve pounder he feels that fate has been kind to him; if not, there is another day and another. However, in the spring of 1979 Pensioners Beach was closed because of the paucity of fish, a sad reminder of the decay of the Columbia River fishery.

The Indian Fishery

In 1957 the Corps of Engineers paid the Indians $27.2 million for their fishing rights at Celilo Falls, which was inundated by The Dalles Dam. Until then the Oregon and Washington fishery agencies had formulated regulations for fishing above Bonneville that were applicable to both Indians and non-Indians alike. After 1957 the area above Bonneville was closed to net fishing, but the tribes were permitted to take salmon for subsistence and ceremonial purposes. For a few years they abided by the ban and then began to sell their increasing catches. Only the Warm Springs Indians, among the four tribes who were paid off, remained faithful to the 1957 agreement.

Efforts by the states to negotiate reasonable settlements with the recalcitrant tribes were unsuccessful, although limited voluntary restraints were adopted by some of them. The issue reached a climax in the summer of 1964 when Indians defied the order forbidding fishing for summer chinook, a run that had already fallen to critical levels. From 1960 to 1965 the Indians increased their catches from 45,000 to 1 million pounds. As a consequence, the Oregon Fish Commission announced in the spring of 1966 its intention to ask the state police to enforce strictly the law forbidding commercial fishing in the upper river. Indians were arrested, but they were usually found not guilty by the courts. In 1968 their lawyers petitioned the U.S. District Court for an injunction to prevent enforcement of state regulations.

The brief filed by George Dysart, assistant regional solicitor of the Department of the Interior in Portland, argued that the tribes did not sell their fishing rights at Celilo Falls but sold "essentially a flowage easement over these areas." In other words, the Indians still had the right guaranteed by the Treaty of Walla Walla in 1855, "to go to the usual and accustomed places to take fish free from interference by the state or others." The only restraints they recognized were those necessary to prevent destruction of the runs, and then only according to regulations they themselves would prescribe. Judge Robert C. Belloni in 1969 *(Sohappy* v. *Smith)* accepted Dysart's arguments and ruled that the state of Oregon "must so regulate the taking of fish that, except for unforeseen circumstances beyond its control, the treaty tribes and their members will be accorded an opportunity to take, at their usual and accustomed fishing places, by reasonable means feasible to them, a fair and equitable share of all the fish which it permits to be taken from any given runs."[7] This ruling opened a can of worms which has since plagued efforts at administering the fishery in a manner that is "fair and equitable" to all user groups, and most of all it has inhibited efforts to save a declining resource.

In 1974 Federal Judge Boldt ruled in a suit filed by Washington tribes regarding fishing on Washington streams that they were entitled to 50 percent of the catchable salmon that would have reached their fishing places. In 1975 Judge Belloni, whose district covers the Columbia River, applied this percentage for the benefit of the Warm Springs, Yakima, Umatilla, and Nez Perce Indians claiming rights on the Columbia. Thus a kind of private and lucrative fishing preserve of 130 miles, from the Bridge of the Gods to the Umatilla River, was handed to the 300 to 400 fishermen benefiting from their treaty rights.

A 1976 news release by the Oregon Department of Fish and Wildlife comments: "The legal decisions have substantially increased the complexity of the management problems facing state agencies. In the course of clarifying basic legal issues, the courts have been interjected into the entire scope of fisheries management. The final results have rarely been satisfactory to either side. By maintaining continuing jurisdiction and preferring to remand rather than resolve, the courts have sought to encourage compromise by the litigants." The Boldt and Belloni decisions have generated a continuous course of litigation by the tribes involved. Their attorneys have filed petitions and suits so frequently that the state agencies have been forced to spend considerable time defending and amending their regulations. The role of the Indians, says the 1976 release, "has been to secure and preserve fishing rights provided by the treaties with the United States. The role of the states . . . has been to balance biological, legal, cultural, political and economic realities of uneven proportions."[8]

Indian catches in the Columbia River (see Fig. 8) hit a peak of 2.8 million pounds in 1975, followed by a drop to 2.7 million in 1976 and 1.6 million in the generally poor year 1977. In recent years their catches have exceeded those at Celilo Falls before The Dalles Dam was built. Indeed, in 1976 the treaty Indians accounted for 46 percent of the total chinook river harvest and 38 percent of all salmonid species—and only 300 to 400 persons participated in the fishery. The conservation instinct of their ancestors has long vanished, and they are as zealous of their rights and attendant economic benefits as the most rugged capitalist.

In 1977 the states of Oregon and Washington made an agreement with the tribes, who fish entirely with setnets in their private preserve on the mid-Columbia, under which for the next five years they would be allocated 40 percent of all harvestable spring chinook and 60 percent of the fall chinook bound for waters above Bonneville Dam. However, the depressed runs in succeeding years made it impossible to fulfill this agreement by the agencies without severely reducing the catches of other user groups. The result has been incessant controversies and appeals by the Indians to their protector, the federal court, which often granted their requests and ordered shorter fishing time for non-Indians.

The Indian fishing rights issue finally reached the U.S. Supreme Court, which, on July 2, 1979, ruled that the 1855 treaty guaranteed the tribes the right to catch an equal share of the harvestable salmon and steelhead in the river at their usual and accustomed fishing places, including fish caught on reservations and for sustenance and ceremonial purposes. Prior to this decision the district courts had ruled that sustenance, ceremonial, and on-reservation catches were not to be counted as part of the Indian share. The minority of the court wrote a dissenting opinion saying there is no basis in the treaties for granting the tribes an "equal share" of the fish, as Judges Boldt and Belloni decreed.

New Directions in Regulation

The Indians, riding the crest of a national wave of Indian assertion of their rights, marked by fish-ins, sit-ins, violent demonstrations, and perpetual litigation, are secure in their victory, but the fight for pieces of the "resource" in the Columbia River grows more bitter among user groups. In 1979 and 1980 state agencies approached the formulation of the next year's fishing regulations convinced that drastic changes had to be made, that curtailment of seasons had to be imposed on all groups. It was clear that too many fishermen were chasing too few fish. Fishing seasons had been steadily curtailed for gillnetters, from 272 to 274 days during World War I to 101 days in 1960, 82 days in 1970, and 52 days in 1978. Oddly enough, although the fishing seasons were drastically reduced, the number of gillnet licenses issued by Oregon and Washington more than doubled between 1969 and 1975.

The sport fishing season both on the ocean and in the rivers was also reduced in 1979. There was an immediate outcry from the charter boat operators as well as from the Indians, who filed a suit asking that regulations be set aside. The commercial trollers claimed that the cut of eight weeks from the previous season was too much and the Indians, in contrast, that the season was too long and would deprive them of fish that normally might reach their nets in the mid-Columbia. As usual, they had their way and a federal judge ordered a substantial reduction in the ocean trolling season.

Higher prices compensated the fishermen for the shorter season. The *Oregonian* on August 7, 1979, reported that "the most successful trollers grossed at least twice the income they had earned for coho at this point in the season over a year ago." The price of salmon at retail hit six dollars a pound, highest on record. Nevertheless some gillnetters decided to abandon the fishery, at least for 1979. In Astoria some of the commercials were converting their boats and gear to take black cod (sablefish) and albacore, shrimp, and crab. "The marginals," the port director at Ilwaco told the *Oregonian*, "are getting hit the hardest." Some trollers and gillnetters decided to fish around Alaska, which was having a record salmon season. The 1980 season for salmon trollers was shorter than in 1979.

The gillnetters were "caught on the hook," so to speak, by the constant reductions in the number of days they could fish. These are the people who live and work in the lower Columbia area, tucked away from the busy highways. "You leave behind the freeway near Longview, Washington," said S. G. Radhuber in the *Oregonian's Northwest Magazine* of February 23, 1975. "You drive past the charming town of Cathlamet, where for $1.50 you can take a nostalgic trip on the only ferry still crossing the Columbia. You are . . . headed for towns named Skamokawa, Gray's River, Naselle, Altoona. The houses thin out. . . . Abandoned creameries, bleached by the foggy tidal air, are all that remain of a collapsed cheese industry. The rotting canneries that have long since moved away dot the river bank, leaving the pilings to the birds. . . . [Finally] you can see the graceful boats of the gillnetters, rocking quietly along the gray, weathered docks."

These people accept fatalistically the steady erosion of their fishing seasons. Gillnetting is for them now usually part-time work, but also a way of life, in some cases inherited from their fathers. Some of them have a job in town, or are getting social security. Some of the younger men like Kent Martin, former president of the fishermen's union, and his wife, take their boats to Alaska when they cannot fish near home. According to Martin:

> Monetarily, inflated prices for salmon have compensated for the decline in catches, so that our income is comparatively the same or higher than 15 years ago. The poundage is probably about 60% of what it was in 1965. Because the upper river stocks are gone, lower

river stocks are now the mainstay of the commercial gillnet fishery, and they are in good shape. However, as many of the local canneries canned only fancy grades of salmon, the destruction of the upper river stocks by dams eliminated their product, which was intended for specialty markets, and they were unable to make the change and went out of business. Local processors thus have suffered more than the fishermen, perhaps, due to the decline in runs. In addition, the summer months are now spent in fisheries far from home, such as Alaska or Puget Sound, whereas they were once spent on the river. There are problems here for families which are split up for one or two months a year, sometimes more, and of course the fishermen lose touch with their local fishing grounds and find it difficult to maintain them on so little fishing time.[9]

If ocean fishing continues to be more and more restricted in the interest of conservation, as is likely, the gillnetters may see better times because more of the harvests will be made in the rivers. No country in the world except Japan, the United States, and Canada permits ocean fishing for salmon that takes large numbers of immature fish that have not reached their full growth, and thus constitutes a wastage of the resource.

CHAPTER 9

Columbia River Salmon and Steelhead Trout:

Endangered Species?

In 1947 Paul Needham of the Oregon Fish Commission predicted that "some of the plans of the dam builders, if completed, will completely ruin for all time some of the richest fishery resources of this nation." On his list were the upper Columbia and Snake rivers and their tributaries. Needham's prophecy is well on its way to becoming true. Much of the resource is irretrievably lost.

The upriver races of spring and summer chinook have reached almost a point of no return; the coho are diminishing; sockeye exist only in token populations; chum have disappeared; only the fall chinook remain relatively abundant. The winter steelhead are holding their own in the lower rivers, but the upper river steelhead are in trouble. In fact, the state agencies that manage the fishery warn that fishing intensity in The Dalles and John Day pools by the Indians must be reduced if the natural upriver races are to continue to produce at a meaningful level.

"It is an inescapable fact that as the mortality of salmon and steelhead due to the dams and other water uses increases," says Leon Verhoeven, "the surplus that is available for harvest decreases."[1] Only the tremendous output of artificially propagated stocks has kept the stocks up to their present greatly reduced levels.

The 1978 and 1979 fishing seasons ended in chaos and bitterness among user groups. For the ocean trollers and river gillnetters 1979 was one of the shortest seasons on record, and for the recreational fisherman the bag limit was reduced from three to two salmon. The treaty Indians with court decisions to support them suffered little if at all. Bad feeling marked the relations of the different groups during the year. Commercial trollers blamed and abused federal and state officials who set the regulations and the Coast Guard who had to enforce them as well as the federal judge who gave the Indians nearly everything they wanted. As the value of salmon rose to six dollars a pound retail, the fight for a piece of the fishery "pie" became more acrimonious. The organized sport fishermen want the non-Indian gillnetters off the river and the commercial troll fishery sharply curtailed. And so it goes.

Taken as a whole, the Columbia River salmon fishery is now but a shadow of what it was before the high dams at Rock Island and Bonneville were built in the 1930s, and by then much of the resource had already been lost through overfishing and habitat degradation.

The Fight for Water

Behind the crisis in the fishery is the fight for that precious commodity—water. The main uses for Columbia River water are (1) to irrigate farmland, (2) to generate power, (3) for navigation by cargo-carrying barges and ships, (4) for direct consumption in homes, factories, shops, and so on, and (5) for the sustenance, migration, spawning, and rearing of fish. Water rights are allocated by the states on the basis of these uses, but so far no minimum flows have been set for migratory fish.

In Europe salmon rivers are usually privately owned. In England the riparian owner also owns the water in the river up to the middle of the stream as well as the fish that come up to his property. He can take all the fish that are catchable by legal means; he may not blockade the stream or pollute it and thus damage the property of other riparian owners. In the United States the rivers are publicly owned and if the stream is navigable, the federal government has the last say; this creates a grab bag for which various groups contend. The states not only may assign water rights but may set minimum flows. The state of Washington is beginning to set minimum flows for some Puget Sound rivers and is formulating a plan for the Columbia River drainage.

About 90 percent of the water that is diverted in the Columbia basin from the river goes to irrigation. About half of these diversions return to the river as runoff, "but where it returns and when is uncertain," says Tom Alkire in his series of articles on the Columbia published in *Willamette Week* (Portland, Oregon) in June 1979. Irrigation water, of course, is reused as it flows past the power dams. Columbia River water now irrigates some 8 million acres in Idaho, Washington, and Oregon, or 25 percent more land than is irrigated by the Nile in Egypt to produce food for 40 million people. When the second phase of the Grand Coulee project is opened to irrigation in 1980, another half-million acres will be added. Meanwhile pressure mounts from agricultural interests to divert more water from the Snake for irrigation, much of which would be used to grow wheat, potatoes, sugar beets, and other crops in surplus supply in the United States.

Power, irrigation, and fishery interests are clashing over the rights to Columbia River water as never before. Water diverted for irrigation may be partly lost for power generation. Power and fishery people argue that no more setasides of water to grow irrigated crops such as wheat, potatoes, and sugar cane are necessary. As Norman Whittlesey, an agricultural economist at Washington State University, told the reporter for *Willamette Week,* "We do not need the food. We are paying several billion dollars a year to keep land out of production, including not only dryland wheat farmers but growers of potatoes and sugar beets."

In the fight for Columbia River water the power interests are dominant. They have been able to persuade the people of the Pacific Northwest that there is an accelerated demand for electricity, requiring a steady increase in generation capacity. Only lip service is paid to conservation. Thus the Bonneville Power Administration has no difficulty getting all the money it claims it needs for building transmission lines and other power facilities and investing staggering sums in nuclear power plants, nor does the Corps of Engineers, whose grandiose plans mesmerize congressional committees, find much opposition to its intention to build additional powerhouses and turbines at its dams. The Bureau of Reclamation also benefits from this happy congressional situation, for it has been constructing a third powerhouse at Grand Coulee Dam since 1970.

The Bonneville Power Administration has for many years been promoting its hydrothermal program. BPA administrators in the 1960s and 1970s predicted dire consequences if the gargantuan amounts of electricity they claimed were needed were not provided on the schedule they set, using annual rates of growth in demand that were wildly exaggerated. Meanwhile they were making contracts with aluminum companies to build additional plants using Columbia River power, a gross defiance of the needs of fisheries for precious water. The plants could have easily located elsewhere but would have had to pay higher rates for power, the main ingredient in the aluminum manufacturing process.

It is well known that the low cost of electricity in the Pacific Northwest has led to overuse and misuse by householders, shops, and factories. A booklet issued by BPA in 1978 says that the average household uses almost twice as much electricity as the national average—15,000 kilowatt-hours per year at 1.5 cents per kilowatt-hour (since considerably increased) compared with 8,000 kilowatt-hours at 3.45 cents in the United States as a whole.[2]

The most profligate use of Columbia River water is to generate electricity for the aluminum mills that have no real reason for locating in the region except for access to bargain-basement rates; the aluminum smelters must bring their raw material, bauxite, from distant countries. In the fiscal year 1977, 36 percent of BPA's total sales of 61.7 billion kilowatt-hours went to the aluminum industry. When one considers some of the end uses of aluminum, such as beer cans, wrapping foil, and the like, the sacrifice of incalculable quantities of salmonids for such nonessential purposes seems like a travesty of common sense.

Because of the demand of the power industry for prior use of the water to maximize generation, the burdens of the migrating fishes have been sometimes unbearably increased. During years of low and even average runoff, there may not be sufficient water in the Columbia and lower Snake to meet the needs of power generation and requirements of young migrating fish. (See Fig. 14.) This situation has been responsible for a large portion of the kills, as in the low-water year 1977.

"The immediate main-stem flow needs of upper Columbia Basin salmon and steelhead," says Ed Chaney in his study, *A Question of Balance,* produced for the Pacific Northwest Regional Commission whose members include the governors of Idaho, Oregon, and Washington, "can be met only by reducing or at least modifying hydrogeneration at main-stem dams in order to free water to flush downstream migrants through reservoirs and over dams."[3] But the power industry has usually been reluctant to do this, arguing that it would jeopardize their ability to meet loads—at the same time that BPA was exporting electricity to California, which in effect means it was exporting water needed by the fish.

According to Chaney, when BPA finally agreed to curtail gener-

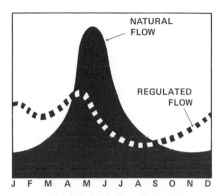

Figure 14. Generalized effect of reservoir operation of Columbia River flows in vicinity of The Dalles, Oregon, during spring runoff; excess use of runoff for power generation slows down migration of juvenile fish from upper basin spawning and rearing areas (source: Chaney, *Question of Balance*)

ation in 1977 for a ten-day period to provide "survival level" flows for young salmonids, its loss was made up in the next six months throughout the coordinated power system of the Pacific Northwest. Every year the fishery agencies have had to negotiate with federal agencies, public utility districts, and private utilities operating power plants on the rivers for arrangements to facilitate fish migration in the spring. The PUDs have been the most recalcitrant of all groups.

An omnibus Pacific Northwest energy bill, shepherded by Senator Henry Jackson of Washington, passed the Senate in 1979 and is now in the House. Spokesmen led by Congressmen Dingell of Michigan and Weaver of Oregon inserted strong language in the bill to protect salmonid migration and to make the utilities liable for compensation for fish losses. At the time of writing the future of this bill is dubious, mainly because of bitter opposition by the utilities to giving the fish a break.

W. G. Hallauer, director of the Washington Department of Ecology, issued a draft of a report on April 1, 1979, entitled *Columbia River Instream Resource Protection Program.* In the letter of conveyance to Governor Ray, he says, "Protection for instream resources should be treated as a higher priority than the production of nonfirm hydroelectric power. . . . Both fisheries flow conditions and future Columbia River irrigation diversions are proposed to be reduced. The intent of this policy is to insure a sharing of the shortage during low water years." What this means is spelled out in the report:

1. Establishment of minimum average daily flows by administrative regulation.

2. Establishment of instantaneous daily flows by administrative regulation. . . . [This] includes a provision for reduction during low water years.

3. Establishment of a conservation cutback provision on future irrigation water rights to insure the sharing of the shortage during low water years.

4. Provision of a volume of water for fish and wildlife by negotiation. The use of this volume is to be determined by the system operators and the fish and wildlife interests. . . .

5. Authorization language for federal projects to include fish and wildlife purposes.

6. Intervention in licensing proceedings to seek flow provisions . . . [to] protect fish and wildlife.[4]

The Department of Ecology also supports "environmentally and economically sound additions" to the storage capacity in the Columbia River system. This would give irrigators more water to compensate for what they might be deprived of when additional flows are needed for fish passage. Finally, the department recommends additional research on the control of reservoir pool fluctuations which result in adverse impacts on fish, wildlife, and recreation—that is, drawdowns for power generation, flood control, and irrigation.

Backing up these recommendations are data published in February 1979 by the Columbia River Fisheries Council in a study called *Rationale for Instream Flows for Fisheries in the Columbia and Snake Rivers.* It quotes results of studies which show that minimum daily average flow is the major variable governing flow-related losses of juvenile salmon and steelhead migrants that have a very critical time schedule in reaching the ocean. Smolt migration must occur in water temperature below 54 degrees F. The smolts usually begin their migration in the Snake River drainage in mid-April and they must reach the open Columbia by mid-May. It takes them about 41 days in moderate flow years to 69 days in low flow years to travel through eight dams and reservoirs. If the temperature goes to 54 degrees or more they may revert to the premigratory stage, and this retards their adjustment to saltwater. The results are mortalities up to 80 percent.[5] In 1977 there was not enough cool water to impel the juvenile chinook and steelhead in the Snake

River to migrate past Lower Monumental Dam. Millions of juveniles had to be transported around the "killer dams" to open water below Bonneville to insure adequate survival. Similar emergency measures were taken in subsequent years.

All this proves that "instream flows," as the biologists call them, are one of the major keys to reducing juvenile mortalities. They now have the data with which to face the power and irrigation people as they demand a fair share of the water for the fish. Implementation of their recommendations on instream flows would probably do more to halt the decline of upriver runs than all other proposed protection measures combined.

New Forestry Attitudes

It is heartening to see that the U.S. Forest Service is taking active steps to safeguard and enhance the anadromous fishes in streams in the national forests. It realizes, as some of its economists and biologists have shown, that in some forests the fisheries are as valuable, or more valuable, than the timber which may be cut from a given tract. Such conclusions were unknown when I worked for the Forest Service during World War II, because wildlife and fisheries were of only remote concern to the foresters. The average forester, it seemed to me then, regarded a well-stocked forest as a wood producer, with water an important but subsidiary resource. He was hardly aware of the fisheries except as they played a role in forest recreation. Now, as Dr. Fred Everest, of the U.S. Forest Service's Northwest Forest and Range Experiment Station, says, "many decisions concerning utilization, allocation, and protection of resources on the forest are made on the basis of perceived economic values."[6] When the biologists can provide estimates of the economic values of the nontimber resources of a forest, a more balanced program of forest management results. Improved management, says Everest, has occurred in three areas: (1) fish habitat protection during timber harvest, (2) land-use planning, and (3) rehabilitation and enhancement of fish habitat.

There is usually a way to obtain desired economic benefits from cutting the timber in an area rich in fish life without unduly impairing the fish resource. Everest offers an example taken from the Rogue River National Forest in southern Oregon to illustrate the most desirable approach to the problem of removing the most streamside trees while providing a high degree of protection for the stream and its fishlife. "This can be accomplished," he says, "by directionally felling riparian timber with jacks and yarding with an aerial skyline system. Residual commercial [trees] are protected; streambank stability is maintained; and the stream channel is not subjected to large increases in sediment and woody debris. . . . These practices increase the cost of felling and yarding . . . but allow removal of about 85% of riparian timber while maintaining about 90% of current fish production. Directional felling also increases yield of riparian timber by about 10% by reducing breakage . . . and is highly cost-effective."[7]

Region 6 of the Forest Service has published statewide comprehensive plans for management of the fish and wildlife in the national forests in Oregon and Washington. "With increasing values and demand for fish," says Charles R. Whitt, biologist for the Mount Hood National Forest, in a letter to me of May 16, 1979, "a concerted effort will be made to provide the best possible management for this resource in our forest management plan as required by the Forest Management Act of 1976. This portion of the plan dealing with fishery resources will be closely coordinated with the Oregon Department of Fish and Wildlife, U.S. Fish and Wildlife Service, and National Marine Fisheries Service to insure inclusion of mutual and compatible goals." The plan "attempts to place fish and wildlife values in perspective, to give an idea of the capability of the land and water to produce fish and wildlife, and to set a course for managing these resources."[8] The program will begin in fiscal 1981 and calls for the expenditure of $15 million during a five-year period.

Where Present Trends Lead

"Coming events cast their shadow before," is a trite saying, but in the twilight of a great fishery there comes to the surface evidence of unhappy events that may occur in the future. Some people predict the ultimate disappearance of nearly all salmon and steelhead above Bonneville Dam; others prophesy a strong revival of the runs if strong steps, outlined in this book, are taken.

In a letter to me dated February 14, 1975, the Corps of Engineers North Pacific Division reported that as of that date $252,851,000 had been expended in fish-passage facilities, research, and other programs at the Corps' dams in existence and under construction, as follows:

Columbia River	$155,235,000
Snake River	88,234,000
Willamette River	9,382,000
Total	$252,851,000

These figures do not include operation and maintenance of fish-passage facilities, costs of the Columbia River Fishery Development Program (estimated in 1975 by the National Marine Fisheries Service at $180 million), costs of fish protection incurred by the public utility districts at their dams in Washington, and by the Bureau of Reclamation and private utilities at their projects. It is safe to say that by 1980 the total investment in all programs to save the Columbia and Snake rivers anadromous fishery was probably in the neighborhood of $500 million—most of it came from the U.S. Treasury (that is, the taxpayers of the country).

Despite this enormous investment, the resource, at least that portion found in the upper part of the watershed, is in grave jeopardy. In April 1978 Herman J. McDevitt, a member of the Pacific Fishery Management Council, requested the National Marine Fisheries Service to determine the status of the spring and summer chinook runs in his home state of Idaho under the Endangered Species Act. This was the first time that most Americans, especially those living outside the Pacific Northwest, learned that some of the anadromous species in the Columbia River were in serious trouble. Subsequently the review was extended to include salmon and steelhead originating above McNary Dam. If it is found that one or more of the upriver species are in danger of extinction, the federal government would be required, as the Endangered Species Act specifies, to develop protective regulations "necessary and advisable for conservation of the species."

Endangered listing would automatically prohibit the taking of the fish until stocks are built back, a process that would take many years. It would also throw a monkey wrench into the operation of upper river hydroelectric projects which, by their usurpation of water flow needed for the migration of fish, helped to bring their stocks to a low pass.

Looking at the future, it is known that management agencies are contemplating more restrictions on harvesting Columbia River

salmon, both in the ocean and in fresh water. The Pacific Marine
Fisheries Commission in 1978 published two studies, *A Comparative
Analysis of Alternatives for Limiting Access to Ocean Recreational Salmon
Fishing* and *A Review of Limited Entry Alternatives for Commercial Salmon
Fisheries.*[9] The first offers 14 alternatives for limiting access to the
salmon by sportsmen, the second summarizes the techniques that
have been used in Alaska, British Columbia, Washington (in Puget
Sound), and other states to curtail access to the commercial fishery;
its parameter is described as "economic efficiency, biological effec-
tiveness, equitable distribution of values and political feasibility."

Seasons for commercial and sport salmon fishing in the ocean in
1980 did not differ much from 1979.

It is reasonably certain, however, that the golden days of unlim-
ited access by charter boats and commercial trollers, provided they
can obtain a license, are over.

In the history of the salmon around the world, the final step
when the fishery is gravely imperiled is to curtail or eliminate
commercial fishing. When General Franco, an ardent salmon angler, became ruler of Spain, he turned over the remaining small
resource to the sport fishermen and banned nets from the rivers;
ocean fishing disappeared. In European countries whose resource
is threatened by offshore netting and in Canada, severe restrictions
have been imposed on this activity in order to increase the escapement and hence the crops of fish. It is clear that at present ocean
fishing takes an excessive toll of the Columbia River stocks and
the state and federal agencies must ease this pressure.

As Richard A. Buck, chairman of Restoration of Atlantic Salmon
in America, who is promoting an international treaty to coordinate
and reduce the harvesting of this species, now at an all-time low,
says: "high seas fishing takes indiscriminately from perhaps the
very river runs needing particular protection, and results in abso-
lutely no rational or effective means of conserving basic stocks or
ensuring adequate escapements for spawning. Proper management
techniques require that harvesting of salmon takes place only at
the mouths of streams or in streams themselves."[10] In this fashion
adequate stocks could be maintained for each river run. Checking
stations and wholesale distribution centers would be established
at strategic points in river systems. Every fish caught would be
tagged with an official stamp, as beef is tagged by the U.S. Department of Agriculture, and it would be illegal to sell salmon unless
it is certified—one means of curtailing the heavy poaching in the

Columbia River streams. It is difficult to predict if such a radical scheme will ever be imposed in the Columbia River fishery, which seems to be managed more on a political than on a biological basis. If it is not, the future will be dismal.

Many years ago, the late Dr. William F. Thompson, founder of the Fisheries Research Institute at the University of Washington, in a lecture said, "If the building of dams for hydroelectric generation, irrigation, navigation, and flood control continues unabated on the Columbia River system, there may always be a salmon or two in the river but no one will be allowed to catch them. They will be museum pieces," like the Atlantic salmon that once thronged the rivers feeding Lake Ontario. If that happens, it will be testimony to the folly of a society that believed the engineers when they jauntily said, "We can have fish and power too!" The stupendous and expensive efforts to save the Columbia River salmon and steelhead will then have been in vain; the fish ladders at the numerous dams will be empty of salmonids, and the upriver races virtually extinct.

Epilogue:

Society and the Salmon

As we look back to the halcyon era of the Columbia River fishery, when salmon was so cheap that it graced the tables of rich and poor alike, while today it sells for six dollars a pound and is a gourmet food only the relatively well to do can afford, we wonder how the transition from abundance to scarcity came about in a mere forty years. Today the quantity of fresh salmon that reaches the consumer markets is so low that every one of them fetches a stupendous price.

The fate of the Columbia fishery mirrors that of many great rivers around the world: the Sacramento and San Joaquin in California, the Connecticut and Penobscot in New England, the Karluk and numerous others in Alaska; the Rhine, probably Europe's most prolific salmon river; the Loire, premier salmon river of France; the Vistula in Poland—all reduced to token populations or fishless.

The basic causes of these staggering losses of valuable food and game fishes are not hard to pinpoint. Nearly everywhere in Europe and North America the salmon prospered until the advent of the Industrial Revolution and its accompanying population explosion and urbanization which impinged on their habitats. As a fishery man commented to me, "More people are a fact of life worldwide, and the Pacific Northwest has been discovered in the past forty years." Population growth which required development of rivers, large-scale cutting of forests that sheltered fish and game, dam building, massive water diversions for agriculture, and pollution of streams, all these combined to ruin the Columbia River fishery, especially in the upper part of a watershed that spreads over seven states and the province of British Columbia.

Behind the forces that destroyed fisheries and wildlife lies a basic change in social attitudes. Primitive folk like the West Coast Indians did not regard fish or game as salable commodities. They venerated their food animals like the salmon that provided the staple of their diet, and this generated an innate sense of conservation. The white men who usurped their lands were bereft of this sense. Their greed knew no bounds, and many stocks were fished almost to extinction long before the Pacific Northwest began to fill up with people during World War II. The prevailing Indian attitude toward the salmon was expressed to me by a Tlingit in Alaska, descendant of chiefs: "The Great Creator, my father told me, sees everything. The undying Creator created the fish for the benefit of the human beings but we must not take them except for food." He added, "In contrast, the white man is a great wastrel. In Sitka they used to destroy three scows of salmon at a time when canneries could not handle them. . . . We were taught it was a sin to kill off the seed stock but the white man killed the seed stock and depleted the rivers." Overfishing and waste were common long before the era of dam building began in the Columbia River watershed.

The Industrial Revolution everywhere wrought changes in man's attitude toward nature. As people moved from rural to urban environments they lost touch with nature. A swift-flowing, meandering stream was regarded by industrialists merely as a source of water power, to turn a mill wheel, generate electricity, and the like, no longer a thing of beauty and source of joy. Major rivers like the Columbia and the Willamette were converted into arteries of commerce, sources of water for domestic, agricultural, and industrial purposes, especially the generation of electricity, and also depositories of sewage and industrial wastes. Society now decreed that the economic values of such rivers were paramount and the aesthetic worthless; the needs of fishes for clean and well-aerated water and adequate flows must be subservient to power, irrigation, and other utilitarian uses.

In the industrialized nations economic progress is worshiped as the ultimate good and in its name rivers are despoiled and ruined, forests that give life and color to the landscape are chopped down, wildlife are driven out or simply slaughtered like the noble coyote in our western states. The land is scarred with ugly cities, towns, and developments like strip mining, and ribboned with roads and highways, not all of them needed. The haunting words of Clarence Pickernell, a Quinault Indian, make little or no sense to most non-Indians:

> This is my land
> From the time of the first moon
> Till the time of the last sun
> It was given to my people. . . .
> I take good care of this land,
> For I am part of it.
> I take good care of the animals,
> For they are my brothers and sisters.
> I take care of the streams and rivers,
> For they clean my land.
> I honor Ocean as my father,
> For he gives me food and a means of travel.
> Ocean knows everything, for he is everywhere. . . .
> He sees much, and knows more.
> He says, "Take care of my sister, Earth,
> She is young and has little wisdom, but much kindness." . . .
> I am forever grateful for this beautiful and bountiful earth.
> God gave it to me
> This is my land.[1]

No sacrifice of the environment and natural resources is deemed too great if it promotes economic progress. This is the credo of politicians, bankers, industrialists, economists, and others who are the real rulers of our lives. The "thermometer" called Gross National Product is their bible and growth is their watchword. Those who are opposed to growth are regarded by them as enemies of society. The loss of natural resources, including fish and wildlife, and environmental degradation are not reckoned in calculating the growth of the Gross National Product. These adverse impacts of growth are indeed seldom mentioned and rarely quantified except by ecologists and environmentalists. As the English magazine *The Ecologist* (July 1971) editorialized: "Most of the politicians of the so-called developing countries insist on industrializing in order to achieve progress, and they think they can do it and avoid the terrible social and ecological problems that industrialized countries are encountering. . . . These are sheer illusions. It is precisely progress that is causing all our problems, and they cannot be solved save by foregoing it."

A fisheries professor asked me in the course of writing this book,

"Where do salmon and steelhead rate? What percentage of our urban society really cares about salmon and steelhead enough to give up a few or any conveniences?"

We can look back over forty years and see that the people of the Pacific Northwest did not care enough to fight for the preservation of these resources. In 1958 I published a book, *Salmon of the Pacific Northwest: Fish vs. Dams,* which concluded that "there is reasonable assurance that the improvement in some of the salmon runs despite the erection of additional dams will be sustained. It will be many years, however, before we shall be in a position to ascertain whether we can have fish runs of the present magnitude and also all the power, flood control, irrigation water and navigation benefits we need." At that time fishery science was in its infancy, but biologists like Paul Needham saw clearly what the ultimate results would be if the rivers were completely dammed. The people of the region, excited about the new industries and job opportunities, among other things, generated by the multipurpose dams, refused to listen to the alarmists.

Thus, when the Corps of Engineers' latest version of the "308 Report" was unveiled in 1952, it contained comments by the U.S. Fish and Wildlife Service flatly warning that the projects proposed for the lower and middle Snake, "if built to the heights suggested, would do serious and irreparable damage to the anadromous fish populations." The report was sent to Congress with the blessings of all the governors in the seven basin states. All the dams the Corps envisioned in the Snake River were not built, but those that were amply bore out the Fish and Wildlife Service's warning.

Another question my fishery professor friend asks is, "In a time when we try to analyze costs and benefits under the National Environmental Protection Act, and in the current state of fishery science, would we still build as many dams or none?" This suggests that perhaps the fishery scientists now have enough political influence vis-à-vis the dam builders to stop projects they deem inimical to the salmon. I do not believe they have.

The juggernaut moves on. Currently the Corps of Engineers is promoting development of the last free-flowing stretch of the Columbia, in the Hanford Reserve area. Here it would like to build Ben Franklin dam (and possibly others), although it admits that "the probable effects [would be] loss of the natural fisheries resource." In the Senate, Senator Warren Magnuson is apparently sponsoring this project; he is chairman of the Senate appropriations committee, and usually has his way. While opponents of Ben Franklin thought they had killed the project, which was in limbo for a decade, Magnuson quietly wangled an appropriation that enabled the Corps to revive it and with this money it is continuing to design the dam, holding workshops, and plugging its merits. Oregon congressman Al Ullman, chairman of the Ways and Means Committee, elected originally as a conservationist, sponsored the appropriation in the House.

While the salmon and steelhead have decreased, exotic species thrive. The ladder count of shad at Bonneville Dam was the largest in history in 1979. Considerable numbers of shad were caught by anglers and treaty Indians (who are permitted to sell their catches). A sport fishery for walleye has also been created in Lake Roosevelt behind Grand Coulee Dam and throughout the main stem to Bonneville Dam.

The number of salmon and steelhead passing Bonneville Dam in 1979 was 25 percent below the average for the preceding ten years. The Fish and Wildlife Department of Oregon said, "The anadromous fish runs were all poor except for shad."

Perhaps our society will some day wake up to the realization that immense quantities of food and game fishes have been bartered away for some of the more dubious benefits of hydroelectricity listed in this book and for diversion of water, needed by the fish, to grow corps that are in excess supply. If that occurs, it will conclude perhaps that we do not need an aluminum industry which takes over one-third of the power generated at the federal dams, nor should blocks of power be sold for the manufacture of pulp and paper, and that to build more dams on the Columbia is sheer lunacy.

Only about 40 percent of the Columbia's 259,000 square miles of watershed is now left as salmon and steelhead habitat, compared with twice that much originally. Once lost, habitat for such fishes is hard to restore, even at great expense.

I have heard biologists say, "Give us more money to build more hatcheries and we will provide more fish." This theory seems highly acceptable to Congress, lavish with the public purse. But recent evidence shows that while more and more artificially bred salmonids are issuing from the hatcheries, neither the numbers returning to their spawning grounds nor the catches are increasing.

These are some of the real issues behind the current crisis in the Columbia River fishery, yet they are rarely if ever mentioned by fishery managers, politicians, sportsmen, commercial fishermen, or Indians. Probably no major fishery in the world has been so abused and overexploited.

Appendix: Supplementary Tables

TABLE 1

Landings of Columbia River Salmon and Steelhead Trout, Excluding Troll Catches, by Species, 1866–1977

(in thousand pounds)

Year	Chinook	Sockeye	Coho	Chum	Steelhead	Total
1866	272	...	...	...	...	272
1867	1,224	...	...	...	...	1,224
1868	1,904	...	...	...	...	1,904
1869	6,800	...	...	...	...	6,800
1870	10,200	...	...	...	...	10,200
1871	13,600	...	...	...	...	13,600
1872	17,000	...	...	...	...	17,000
1873	17,000	...	...	...	...	17,000
1874	23,800	...	...	...	...	23,800
1875	25,500	...	...	...	...	25,500
1876	30,600	...	...	...	...	30,600
1877	25,840	...	...	...	...	25,840
1878	31,280	...	...	...	...	31,280
1879	32,640	...	...	...	...	32,640
1880	36,040	...	...	...	...	36,040
1881	37,400	...	...	...	...	37,400
1882	36,808	...	...	...	...	36,808
1883	42,799	...	...	...	...	42,799
1884	42,160	...	...	...	...	42,160
1885	37,658	...	...	...	...	37,658
1886	30,498	...	...	...	...	30,498
1887	24,208	...	...	...	...	24,208
1888	25,328	...	...	...	...	25,328
1889	18,135	1,211	...	...	1,727	21,073

1890	22,821	3,899	⋯	⋯	2,912	29,632
1891	24,066	1,053	⋯	⋯	2,010	27,129
1892	23,410	4,525	284	⋯	4,920	33,139
1893	19,637	2,071	1,979	157	4,435	28,279
1894	23,875	2,979	2,908	⋯	3,565	33,327
1895	30,253	1,225	6,773	1,530	3,378	43,159
1896	25,224	1,155	2,999	⋯	3,377	32,755
1897	29,867	882	4,137	⋯	3,138	38,024
1898	23,180	4,554	4,449	⋯	1,787	33,970
1899	18,771	1,630	2,013	774	816	24,004
1900	19,245	895	3,055	1,203	1,401	25,799
1901		⋯	⋯	⋯	⋯	⋯
1902	23,034	1,159	716	707	584	26,200
1903	27,917	570	828	680	493	30,488
1904	31,783	878	2,125	1,407	671	36,864
1905	33,029	528	1,824	1,751	668	37,800
1906	29,971	531	2,818	1,891	442	35,653
1907	24,250	374	2,159	1,534	403	28,720
1908	19,743	584	2,137	1,148	729	24,341
1909	17,119	1,704	2,868	1,688	1,175	24,554
1910	25,326	424	4,687	4,525	370	35,332
1911	36,602	407	5,400	3,636	584	46,629
1912	21,388	558	2,165	1,272	2,147	27,530
1913	19,384	758	2,786	905	2,168	26,001
1914	25,409	2,401	4,744	3,351	1,908	37,813
1915	32,127	371	2,267	5,884	2,690	43,339
1916	31,992	257	3,542	5,288	1,581	42,660
1917	29,552	542	4,372	3,649	2,233	40,348
1918	29,249	2,573	6,674	2,C30	3,023	43,549
1919	30,325	494	6,170	5,133	1,900	44,022

Year	Chinook	Sockeye	Coho	Chum	Steelhead	Total
1920	31,094	178	1,838	1,278	1,166	35,554
1921	21,552	411	2,388	328	1,021	25,700
1922	17,915	2,091	6,150	601	2,163	28,920
1923	21,578	2,605	6,965	1,735	2,684	35,567
1924	22,365	501	7,796	3,927	3,193	37,782
1925	26,660	384	7,937	3,795	2,907	41,683
1926	21,241	1,478	6,606	2,234	3,843	35,402
1927	24,011	468	5,209	4,656	3,147	37,491
1928	18,149	327	3,723	8,497	2,160	32,856
1929	18,151	685	6,701	3,714	2,871	32,122
1930	20,079	668	7,737	773	2,404	31,661
1931	21,378	281	2,714	239	2,126	26,738
1932	16,001	190	4,097	1,174	1,432	22,894
1933	19,528	471	2,702	1,659	1,958	26,318
1934	18,788	467	4,775	1,663	1,919	27,612
1935	15,206	46	2,684	810	1,764	20,510
1936	15,960	302	1,739	1,142	2,304	21,447
1937	18,653	335	1,842	1,910	1,933	24,673
1938	12,418.5	424.6	2,311.0	1,915.4	1,764.4	18,833.9
1939	13,498.8	269.8	1,529.7	1,174.4	1,438.5	17,911.2
1940	13,516.1	361.9	1,373.2	1,253.5	2,815.4	19,320.1
1941	23,238.5	505.7	1,045.0	4,149.8	2,663.7	31,602.7
1942	18,679.1	192.4	64	5,191.1	1,839.1	26,546.2
1943	11,426.5	146.1	706.3	959.9	1,514.5	14,753.3
1944	14,059.6	54.8	1,533.3	275.4	1,720.1	17,643.2
1945	12,972.1	8.7	1,835.5	588.8	1,963.5	17,368.6
1946	14,277.8	128.5	1,059.6	886.6	1,725.6	18,078.1
1947	17,302.7	718.3	1,498.1	496.2	1,648.7	21,664.0
1948	17,352.3	95.8	1,174.7	1,044.8	1,579.0	21,246.6
1949	10,768.5	24.0	899.2	545.0	814.0	13,050.7

Year						
1950	10,421.7	169.2	1,048.0	700.2	964.8	13,303.9
1951	10,036.3	169.4	968.0	532.3	1,207.2	12,913.2
1952	7,271.1	608.7	1,074.0	308.6	1,461.9	10,724.3
1953	6,966.6	146.2	457.5	249.2	1,901.0	9,720.5
1954	5,312.7	243.4	303.4	320.0	1,467.5	7,647.0
1955	8,581.9	200.4	598.8	125.6	1,297.5	10,804.2
1956	8,178.5	287.1	460.0	45.7	811.8	9,783.1
1957	5,918.9	240.2	390.7	32.1	741.1	7,323.0
1958	6,434.0	723.5	167.6	89.3	699.9	8,114.3
1959	4,594.3	635.8	119.5	42.9	672.6	6,065.1
1960	3,928.0	394.1	159.1	15.3	722.5	5,219.0
1961	4,160.2	158.0	382.6	17.3	715.7	5,433.8
1962	5,467.3	51.7	600.0	48.1	723.4	6,890.5
1963	4,346.1	48.8	501.1	15.3	972.2	5,883.5
1964	4,484.0	68.2	1,963.5	23.9	425.0	6,964.6
1965	6,142.9	22.9	1,901.8	6.1	510.1	8,583.8
1966	3,612.2	17.2	4,389.1	11.0	393.3	8,422.8
1967	4,974.1	195.1	3,817.9	9.7	445.2	9,442.0
1968	4,097.1	89.6	962.2	3.4	427.5	5,579.8
1969	5,775.9	104.5	1,663.3	4.0	490.3	8,038.0
1970	6,461.7	55.7	5,745.6	8.0	308.4	12,579.4
1971	5,967.2	285.6	2,277.9	5.9	467.5	9,004.1
1972	5,684.6	275.6	1,239.4	16.0	667.1	7,882.7
1973	8,552.4	15.9	1,904.7	18.0	634.1	11,125.1
1974	3,638.0	....	2,432.0	11.0	185.0	6,266.0
1975	6,587.0	....	1,581.0	6.0	70.0	8,244.0
1976	5,587.0	....	1,328.0	17.0	87.0	7,019.0
1977	4,692.0	....	317.0	2.0	387.0	5,398.0

TABLE 2

SALMONID FISH COUNTED OVER BONNEVILLE DAM, 1938–78

Year	Chinook	Steelhead	Sockeye	Coho	Chum	Pink	Total Salmonids
1938	271,799	107,003	75,040	15,185	2,117	...	471,144
1939	286,189	122,032	73,382	14,383	1,168	...	497,154
1940	391,587	185,174	148,807	11,917	1,729	...	739,214
1941	461,443	118,089	65,741	17,911	5,269	4	668,457
1942	401,942	151,800	55,464	12,402	1,865	11	623,484
1943	313,123	92,133	39,845	2,547	788	...	448,436
1944	240,764	100,518	15,072	4,207	954	1	361,516
1945	297,478	120,133	9,501	790	728	1	428,631
1946	446,052	142,807	74,376	3,898	1,178	2	668,313
1947	480,377	135,444	171,139	11,174	199	3	798,336
1948	419,555	139,062	131,541	4,081	3,636	2	697,877
1949	277,697	119,285	51,444	1,004	2,028	6	451,464
1950	357,375	114,087	77,993	10,151	1,069	8	560,683
1951	331,788	140,689	169,428	5,201	1,044	7	648,157
1952	420,879	260,990	184,645	7,768	1,505	9	875,796
1953	332,479	223,914	235,215	13,018	1,728	10	806,364
1954	320,947	176,260	130,107	4,062	1,569	4	632,949
1955	359,853	198,411	237,748	3,725	318	9	800,064
1956	300,917	131,116	156,418	6,127	693	4	595,275
1957	403,286	139,183	82,915	4,675	569	12	630,640
1958	426,419	131,437	122,389	3,673	455	6	684,379
1959	345,028	129,026	86,560	2,695	906	22	564,237

Year							
1960	256,049	113,676	59,713	3,268	1,026	...	433,732
1961	281,980	139,719	17,111	3,456	896	12	443,174
1962	286,625	164,025	28,179	14,788	1,013	27	494,657
1963	278,560	129,418	60,319	12,658	739	34	481,728
1964	344,422	117,252	99,856	53,602	632	45	615,809
1965	317,957	166,453	55,125	76,032	496	64	616,127
1966	340,111	143,661	156,661	71,891	872	58	713,254
1967	366,237	121,872	144,158	96,488	352	50	729,157
1968	341,154	106,974	108,207	63,488	79	21	619,923
1969	507,543	140,782	59,636	49,378	143	86	757,568
1970	384,780	113,510	70,762	80,116	209	150	649,527
1971	405,702	193,966	87,447	75,989	29	176	763,309
1972	394,456	185,886	56,323	65,932	1	51	702,649
1973	398,635	157,823	58,979	54,609	43	12	670,101
1974	366,759	137,054	43,837	60,955	23	2	608,630
1975	425,566	85,540	58,212	58,307	11	309	627,945
1976	507,773	124,177	43,611	53,150	11	2	728,724
1977	366,657	193,437	99,829	19,408	17	...	679,348
1978	394,600	104,431	18,436	52,590	28	...	570,085
Total	14,852,543	5,818,249	3,721,171	1,126,699	38,135	1,220	25,558,017
41-Year Average	362,257	141,909	90,760	27,480			623,366

SOURCE: U.S. Army Corps of Engineers, North Pacific Division, *Annual Fish Passage Report, Columbia River Project*, Portland, Oregon, 1979.

TABLE 3
Columbia River Canned Salmon Pack, 1940–77
(all data on basis of 48-pound cases)

Year	Plants	Chinook		Blueback (Sockeye)		Silverside (Coho)		Chum and Pink		Steelhead		Total	
		Cases	Value	Cases	Value	Cases	Value	Cases	Value	Cases	Value	Cases	Value
1940	11	244,570	$3,785,681	23,974	$471,530	59,737	$623,681	25,282	$125,420	33,436	$373,514	386,999	$5,379,8
1941	11	328,609	5,558,254	33,070	661,400	35,727	481,834	83,144	572,994	33,162	453,502	513,712	7,727,9
1942	12	274,750	5,692,929	23,256	624,230	26,541	497,070	118,051	911,538	21,803	429,678	464,401	8,156,4
1943	11	130,373	3,094,505	2,880	77,586	5,707	61,065	12,439	112,421	16,261	323,874	167,660	3,669,4
1944	10	163,047	3,714,591	758	20,342	12,210	137,072	1,525	11,590	19,222	375,838	196,762	4,259,4
1945	8	132,014	3,095,228	112	3,001	22,154	244,060	1,032	8,848	19,314	363,068	175,670	3,723,4
1946	11	159,872	5,940,740	9,726	369,588	6,883	206,490	15,617	247,392	17,373	510,720	209,471	7,274,9
1947	10	250,318	8,613,000	15,079	664,000	42,789	1,278,000	17,121	252,000	21,999	650,000	347,306	11,457,0
1948	12	235,310	9,342,000	3,339	147,000	39,425	1,099,000	26,201	498,000	19,977	615,000	324,242	11,701,0
1949	12	133,347	3,682,000	6,630	225,000	16,740	415,000	12,386	186,000	9,019	221,000	178,122	4,729,0
1950	11	136,635	4,964,201	3,630	146,687	29,507	939,296	12,952	234,457	10,266	360,830	192,990	6,645,4
1951	10	143,046	5,497,305	4,552	186,543	29,099	841,234	11,566	192,850	14,862	468,615	203,125	7,187,5
1952	9	95,353	3,506,181	9,824	413,774	29,701	875,380	13,759	214,837	18,979	612,987	167,616	5,623,1
1953	8	97,320	3,267,303	3,014	127,791	24,219	676,237	9,775	130,062	19,420	616,621	153,748	4,818,0
1954	8	71,993	2,550,257	8,485	336,212	12,670	367,000	12,530	190,484	13,379	458,303	119,057	3,902,2
1955	8	117,882	4,392,455	3,010	131,890	20,254	667,659	6,774	126,875	13,737	462,857	161,557	5,781,7
1956	8	112,076	4,328,650	19,346	845,006	22,031	656,182	5,497	130,233	8,171	295,294	167,121	6,255,4
1957	8	87,420	3,738,912	8,496	470,061	28,725	1,024,847	5,770	121,542	7,605	287,028	138,016	5,642,3
1958	7	82,786	3,714,465	44,129	2,144,087	9,917	370,072	6,113	109,862	6,313	229,786	149,258	6,568,2
1959	10	70,149	2,942,503	18,069	823,850	14,931	586,739	6,250	127,751	9,847	356,835	118,246	4,837,6

1960	8	50,285	2,323,334	8,650	496,451	5,202	244,344	2,459	56,166	6,174	275,303	72,770	3,400.62
1961	8	56,351	2,754,543	4,463	259,724	24,72?	1,124,473	3,675	108,784	6,839	327,862	96,051	4,575.38
1962	8	64,437	3,098,600	1,289	72,534	15,178	599,361	5,355	109,600	5,785	234,211	92,044	4,114.30
1963	8	52,213	2,399,052	2,583	142,818	17,299	727,394	2,625	47,667	7,654	326,085	82,374	3,643.01
1964	8	52,620	2,328,838	3,038	190,067	30,478	1,198,947	2,090	37,014			88,226	3,754.86
1965	8	72,550	3,398,776	1,257	69,852	46,216	1,764,154	3,701	100,341	3,747	151,672	127,471	5,484.79
1966	7	42,099	1,963,431	3,466	219,967	51,586	2,094,748	184	4,408	2,875	122,289	100,210	4,404.84
1967	6	42,768	1,986,935	5,086	258,119	48,612	2,100,202	7,438	227,208	2,072	94,599	105,476	4,667.06
1968	6	25,678	1,154,724	4,385	250,006	26,778	1,184,893	1,602	42,337	2,846	120,651	61,290	2,752.61
1969	5	29,057	1,391,758	6,627	376,319	10,452	435,898	8,222	298,231	2,994	108,245	57,352	2,610.45
1970	6	21,025	1,221,968	1,910	118,894	38,694	1,929,263	4,469	126,724	254	14,718	66,356	3,421.56
1971	8	38,247	1,648,848	37,007	2,123,869	45,573	1,904,935	32,634	1,152,241	2,495	94,713	155,956	6,924.60
1972	7	23,358	1,363,540	5,608	420,600	7,753	298,696	3,697	152,150	1,122	52,734	41,538	2,287.72
1973	8	13,064	1,384,784	1,430	160,160	13,691	1,437,555	6,028	391,820	915	96,990	35,128	3,471.30
1974	8	18,727	1,441,979	220	18,700	35,194	2,991,490	5,855	385,580	1,409	140,900	61,405	4,978.64
1975	6	4,528	401,860	728	65,520	414	33,120	115	7,475			5,785	507.97
1976	6	4,129	442,274	44	4,180	3,846	338,448	561	35,343	2	195	8,578	820.44
1977	7	1,559	149,664	119	7,021	281	15,736	588	25,904			2,547	198.32

SOURCE: *Pacific Packers Report, 1978. National Fisherman.*

Notes

CHAPTER 1
The Pristine River

1. From the memoirs of Francis A. Seufert, last president of the Seufert Canning Company, scheduled to be published by the Oregon Historical Society.

2. John Davies, *Douglas of the Forests: The North American Journals of David Douglas* (Seattle: University of Washington Press, 1980), p. 52.

3. Ibid. p. 58.

4. John K. Townsend, *Narrative of a Journey Across the Rocky Mountains to the Columbia River,* in vol. 21 of *Early Western Travels, 1748–1846,* ed. Reuben Gold Thwaites (Cleveland: Arthur H. Clark Co., 1905), p. 278.

CHAPTER 2
The Indian Fisheries

1. *Journals of Lewis and Clark,* ed. Bernard DeVoto (Boston: Houghton Mifflin Co., 1953), pp. 251–53.

2. William Morwood, *Traveler in a Vanished Landscape: The Life and Times of David Douglas* (New York: Clarkson N. Potter, 1973), p. 63.

3. Alexander Ross, *Adventures of the First Settlers on the Oregon or Columbia River,* vol. 7 of *Early Western Travels, 1748–1846,* ed. Reuben Gold Thwaites (Cleveland: Arthur H. Clark Co., 1904), pp. 296–97.

4. *Journals of Lewis and Clark,* p. 262.

5. Charles Wilkes, *Narrative of the United States Exploring Expedition, during the Years 1838–1842,* 2 vols. (London: Ingram, Cooke, and Co., 1852), 2:184–85.

6. Philip Drucker, *Indians of the Northwest Coast* (Garden City, N.Y.: Natural History Press, 1963), pp. 154–55.

7. *Journals of Lewis and Clark,* p. 358.

CHAPTER 3
The Fisheries in an Age of Abundance

1. Martha Ferguson McKeown, *The Trail Led North: Mont Hawthorne's Story* (Portland, Oreg.: Binfords and Mort, 1960), p. 1.

2. This account of the Seufert cannery is taken from Francis A. Seufert's unpublished memoirs with the kind permission of Mrs. Gladys Seufert.

3. Ivan J. Donaldson and Frederick K. Cramer, *Fishwheels of the Columbia* (Portland, Oreg.: Binfords and Mort, 1971), p. 83.

159

4. The material on Indian fishing gear is taken from Joseph A. Craig and Robert L. Hacker, *The History and Development of the Fisheries of the Columbia River* (Washington, D.C.: U.S. Bureau of Fisheries, Bulletin no. 32, 1940), p. 169.

5. Henry O. Wendler, *Regulation of Commercial Fishing Gear and Seasons on the Columbia River from 1859 to 1963* (Olympia, Wash.: Department of Fisheries, Fisheries Research Papers, vol. 2, no. 4, December 1966).

6. Willis H. Rich, *The Present State of the Columbia River Salmon Resources,* Oregon Fish Commission, Contribution no. 3 (Salem: State Printing Department, 1941), p. 40.

CHAPTER 4
Life History of the Salmon and Steelhead Trout

1. J. M. Macfarlane, *The Evolution and Distribution of Fishes* (New York: Macmillan, 1923).

2. See G. V. Nikolsky, *The Ecology of Fishes* (New York: Academic Press, 1963).

3. R. E. Foerster, *The Sockeye Salmon,* Research Bulletin 162 (Ottawa: Fisheries Research Board of Canada, 1968), p. 67.

4. Lynwood Smith, personal communication.

5. See Anthony Netboy, *The Salmon: Their Fight for Survival* (Boston: Houghton Mifflin Co., 1974), pp. 15–21, for a detailed discussion of Pacific salmon ocean migrations.

6. Donald Chapman, "The Life History of the Alsea River Steelhead," *Journal of Wildlife Management* 22 (April 1958).

7. Ferris Neave, "Ocean Migrations of Pacific Salmon," *Journal of the Fisheries Research Board of Canada* 21, no. 5 (September 1964): 1239–40.

8. William F. Royce, Lynwood Smith, and Alan C. Hartt, *Models of Oceanic Migrations of Pacific Salmon and Comments on Guidance Mechanisms,* Fishery Bulletin 63 (3) (Washington, D.C.: U.S. Fish and Wildlife Service, 1968).

9. Leon Verhoeven, personal communication.

10. Brian Curtis, *The Life Story of the Fish* (New York: Harcourt, Brace, 1961), pp. 197–98.

11. This account of the spawning process is based on Leonard P. Schultz, "The Breeding Habits of Salmon and Trout," *Smithsonian Report for 1937,* reprinted in *Earth and Life,* vol. 2 of *Smithsonian Treasury of Science,* ed. Webster P. True (New York: Simon and Schuster, 1960), pp. 593–609.

CHAPTER 5
Alteration of the Watershed and Its Consequences

1. John H. Storer, *The Web of Life: A First Book of Ecology* (New York: Devin-Adair Co., 1954), p. 107.

2. Marston Bates, *The Forest and the Sea* (New York: Random House, 1960), pp. 87–88.

3. See Bernard Frank and Anthony Netboy, *Water, Land, and People* (New York: Alfred A. Knopf, 1950), pp. 56–89.

4. Theodore Roosevelt, *An Autobiography* (New York: Scribner's, 1923), p. 398.

5. Bureau of Reclamation, *The Columbia River: A Comprehensive Report on the Development of the Water Resources of the Columbia River Basin for Review Prior to Submission to the Congress* (Washington, D.C.: U.S. Government Printing Office, 1947), p. 356.

6. Jack Shepherd, *The Forest Killers* (New York: Weybright and Talley, 1975), p. 116.

7. Ibid., p. 152.

8. Ibid., p. 149.

9. G. A. Holland, J. E. Lasater, E. D. Neumann, and W. E. Eldridge, *Toxic Effects*

of Organic and Inorganic Pollutants on Young Salmon and Trout, Research Bulletin no. 5 (Olympia: Washington Department of Fisheries, September 1960).

10. Federal Water Pollution Control Administration, "Summary of Water Quality Control and Management, Willamette River Basin," Portland, Oregon, January 1967.

11. See Annual Report, "Fish Passage at Willamette Falls" (Portland: Oregon Department of Fish and Wildlife, March 1979).

CHAPTER 6

The Killer Dams

1. E. F. Fish and Mitchell G. Hanavan, *A Report Upon the Grand Coulee Fish-Maintenance Project, 1939–1947,* U.S. Fish and Wildlife Service, Special Scientific Report no. 55, November 1958.

2. This statement was obtained from the late Francis Seufert, last president of the Seufert Canning Company. No written or published version of the statement has come to light; probably it was orally circulated in the Pacific Northwest. The Corps of Engineers, of course, denies that the statement was ever made.

3. C. H. Clay, *Design of Fishways and Other Fish Facilities* (Ottawa: Department of Fisheries of Canada, 1961), p. 57.

4. Ralph Silliman, *Fluctuations in Abundance of Columbia River Chinook Salmon, 1939–1945,* U.S. Fish and Widlife Service, Fishery Bulletin 514, 1950.

5. Columbia Basin Inter-agency Committee, *Minutes of the Tenth Meeting,* Walla Walla, Washington, June 25–26, 1947.

6. Paul R. Needham, "Dams Threaten West Coast Fisheries Industry," *Oregon Business Review* 6, no. 6 (June 1947): 1, 3–4.

7. U.S. Congress, Subcommittee of the Committee on Appropriations, *Hearings,* 83d Cong., 1st sess., part 1.

8. Elizabeth Drew, "Dam Outrage: The Story of the Army Corps of Engineers," in *Who Needs Nature?* ed. Dixie S. Jackson (New York: John Wiley, 1973). See also Arthur E. Morgan, *Dams and Other Disasters: A Century of the Army Corps of Engineers in Civil Works* (Boston: Porter Sargent, 1971), and George Laycock, "The Dam Shame: It's Still with Us," *Outdoor Life,* June 1979.

9. For a more complete discussion of the 1952 "308 Report" see Anthony Netboy, "Impact of Non-Fish Uses of the Columbia River," in *Columbia River Salmon and Steelhead,* ed. Ernest Schwiebert (Washington, D.C.: American Fisheries Society, 1977), pp. 196–201.

10. See Anthony Netboy, *Salmon of the Pacific Northwest: Fish vs. Dams* (Portland, Oreg.: Binfords and Mort, 1958), p. 89.

11. Federal Power Commission, *Initial and Reply Brief of Commission Staff Counsel,* Snake River Dams, Washington, D.C., October 22, 1970.

12. Clay, *Design of Fishways,* p. 57.

13. From notes taken by the author.

14. Wesley J. Ebel, "Major Passage Problems," in *Columbia River Salmon and Steelhead,* pp. 33–34.

15. For recent trends in the Snake River runs, see "The Snake River Salmon and Steelhead Crisis" (Seattle: National Marine Fisheries Service, Northwest Fisheries Center, February 1975).

16. Wesley J. Ebel and Howard L. Raymond, "Effect of Atmosphere Gas Supersaturation on Salmon and Steelhead Trout of the Snake and Columbia Rivers," *Marine Fisheries Review,* July 1976.

17. Leon Verhoeven, personal communication.

18. Ed Chaney, *A Question of Balance: Water/Energy—Salmon and Steelhead Production in the Columbia River Basin* (Eagle, Idaho: Northwest Resources Information Center, 1978).

CHAPTER 7
The Compensation Programs

1. Ernest Jeffries, director of hatcheries, Oregon Department of Fish and Wildlife, June 1978, personal communication.
2. Roger E. Burrows and Bobby D. Combs, "Controlled Environments for Salmon Propagation," *Progressive Fish Culturist* 30, no. 3 (July 1968): 123.
3. Roger E. Burrows, "The Influence of Fingerling Quality on Adult Salmon Survivals," *Transactions of the American Fisheries Society* 98, no. 4 (October 1969): 777–84.
4. See Fred Cleaver, "Role of Hatcheries in the Management of Columbia River Salmon," in *Columbia River Salmon and Steelhead,* ed. Ernest Schwiebert, p. 91.
5. Stephen W. Pettit, "Compensation and What It Means to Idaho," ibid., p. 171.
6. James B. Haas, "Compensation for Salmon and Steelhead Losses on the Columbia River System," ibid., pp. 177–78.

CHAPTER 8
The Fisheries in an Age of Scarcity

1. Oregon Department of Fish and Wildlife, *Maximizing the Return of Salmon and Steelhead to Oregon Fisheries,* a Report to the 1977 Oregon Legislature, January 1977.
2. Robert Gunsolus, "Status of the Salmon and Steelhead Runs Entering the Columbia River," in *Columbia River Salmon and Steelhead,* ed. Ernest Schwiebert, p. 22.
3. Ibid.
4. Ibid.
5. Dame Juliana Berners, *The Origins of Angling, and a new printing of A Treatise of Fishing with an Angle,* ed. John McDonald (Garden City, N.Y.: Doubleday, 1963).
6. Oregon Department of Fish and Wildlife, *Willamette Basin Fish Management Report,* March 1, 1979.
7. See Herb Williams and Walt Neubrach, *Indian Treaties: American Nightmare* (Seattle: Outdoor Empire Publishing, Inc., 1977), pp. 36–38.
8. *Maximizing the Return of Salmon and Steelhead to Oregon Fisheries.*
9. Kent Martin, personal communication, August 27, 1979.

CHAPTER 9
Columbia River Salmon and Steelhead Trout: Endangered Species?

1. Leon Verhoeven, personal communication.
2. Bonneville Power Administration, *Fiscal Year 1977, Financial and Statistical Summary, Columbia River Power System* (Portland, Oreg.: Department of Energy, 1978).
3. Chaney, *A Question of Balance,* p. 17.
4. Washington Department of Ecology, *Columbia River Instream Resource Protection Program* (Olympia, March 1, 1979).
5. Columbia River Fisheries Council, *Rationale for Instream Flows for Fisheries in the Columbia and Snake Rivers* (Portland, Oreg., February 1979), pp. 4–6.
6. Fred H. Everest, "Anadromous Fish Habitat and Forest Management—Economic Considerations," in *Western Proceedings: Fifty-eighth Annual Conference of the Western Association of Fish and Wildlife Agencies* (San Diego, Calif., July 17–20, 1978), p. 159.
7. Ibid., p. 161.
8. U.S. Forest Service, Region 6, *Statewide Comprehensive Plan for Fish and Wildlife in the National Forests in the State of Washington* (Portland, Oreg., November 1978), p. 4.
9. Frank J. Hester and Philip E. Sorensen, *A Comparative Analysis of Alternatives for Limiting Access to Ocean Recreational Salmon Fishing* (Portland, Oreg.: Pacific Marine

Fisheries Commission, April 1978), and Russell G. Porter, *A Review of Limited Entry Alternatives for Commercial Salmon Fisheries* (June 1978).

10. Personal communication, September 25, 1979. See also Anthony Netboy, *Salmon: The World's Most Harassed Fish* (London: Andre Deutsch, 1980), p. 203.

Epilogue

1. Quoted from *Uncommon Controversy: Fishing Rights of the Muckleshoot, Puyallup, and Nisqually Indians,* a report prepared for the American Friends Service Committee (Seattle and London: University of Washington Press, 1969), p. v.

Bibliography

Ashworth, William. *Hells Canyon: The Deepest Gorge on Earth*. New York: Hawthorn Books, 1977.

Ayerst, Jack D. "The Role of Hatcheries in Rebuilding Steelhead Runs of the Columbia River System." In *Columbia River Salmon and Steelhead*, edited by Ernest Schwiebert, pp. 84–88. Washington, D.C.: American Fisheries Society, 1977.

Bentley, Wallace W., and Raymond, Howard L. "Passage of Juvenile Fish Through Orifices in Gatewells of Turbine Intakes at McNary Dam." *Transactions of the American Fisheries Society* 98, no. 4 (October 1969): 723–27.

Bonneville Power Administration. *Fiscal Year 1977, Financial and Statistical Summary, Columbia River Power System*. Portland, Oreg.: Department of Energy, 1978.

Brett, J. R. "The Swimming Energetics of Salmon." *Scientific American*, August 1965, pp. 80–85

Burrows, Roger E. "The Influence of Fingerling Quality on Adult Salmon Survivals." *Transactions of the American Fisheries Society* 98, no. 4 (October 1969): 777–84.

Burrows, Roger E., and Combs, Bobby D. "Controlled Environments for Salmon Propagation." *Progressive Fish Culturist* 30, no. 3 (July 1968): 123–36.

Chaney, Ed. *A Question of Balance: Water/Energy—Salmon and Steelhead Production in the Columbia River Basin*. Eagle, Idaho: Northwest Resources Information Center, 1978.

Clark, Ella E. *Indian Legends of the Pacific Northwest*. Berkeley: University of California Press, 1953.

Clay, C. H. *Design of Fishways and Other Fish Facilities*. Ottawa: Department of Fisheries of Canada, 1961.

Cleaver, Fred. "Role of Hatcheries in the Management of Columbia River Salmon." In *Columbia River Salmon and Steelhead*, edited by Ernest Schwiebert, pp. 89–92. Washington, D.C.: American Fisheries Society, 1977.

Cobb, John W. *Pacific Salmon Fisheries*. Appendix 3 of *Report of the U.S. Commissioner of Fisheries*. Bulletin 1. Washington, D.C., 1940.

165

166   *Bibliography*

Columbia Basin Inter-agency Committee. *Minutes of the Tenth Meeting.* June 25–26, 1947.

Columbia River Fisheries Council. *Rationale for Instream Flows for Fisheries in the Columbia and Snake Rivers.* Portland, Oregon, February 1979.

The Columbia River: A Comprehensive Report on the Development of the Water Resources of the Columbia River Basin for Review Prior to Submission to the Congress. Bureau of Reclamation, Department of the Interior. Washington, D.C.: U.S. Government Printing Office, 1947.

Columbia River Fish Runs and Commercial Fisheries, 1938–1970: 1973 Addendum. Vol. 1, no. 4 (January 1974). Oregon Fish Commission.

Columbia River Fish Runs and Fisheries, 1957–1977. Vol. 2, no. 3 (December 1978). Oregon Fish and Wildlife Department and Washington Department of Fisheries.

Columbia River Salmon and Steelhead. Proceedings of a Symposium Held in Vancouver, Washington, March 5–6, 1976, edited by Ernest Schwiebert. Special Publications no. 10. Washington, D.C.: American Fisheries Society, 1977.

Combs, Trey. *The Steelhead Trout.* Portland, Oreg.: Northwest Salmon Trout Steelheader Co., 1971.

Craig, Joseph A., and Hacker, Robert L. *The History and Development of the Fisheries of the Columbia River.* U.S. Bureau of Fisheries, Bulletin 32. Washington, D.C.: U.S. Government Printing Office, 1940.

Cressman, L. S. *The Sandal and the Cave: The Indians of Oregon.* Portland, Oreg.: Beaver Books, 1964.

Cunningham, Glenn. "Oregon's First Salmon Canner, 'Captain' John West." *Oregon Historical Quarterly* 54, no. 3 (September 1953): 240–48.

Curtis, Brian. *The Life Story of the Fish.* New York: Harcourt, Brace and Co., 1949; Dover, 1961.

Donaldson, Ivan J., and Cramer, Frederick K. *Fishwheels of the Columbia.* Portland, Oreg.: Binfords and Mort, 1971.

Drew, Elizabeth. "Dam Outrage: The Story of the Corps of Army Engineers." In *Who Needs Nature?* edited by Dixie S. Jackson. New York: John Wiley, 1973.

Drucker, Philip. *Cultures of the North Pacific Coast.* San Francisco: Chandler Publishing Co., 1965.

DuPuy, William Atherton. *The Nation's Forests.* New York: Macmillan, 1938.

Ebel, Wesley J., and Raymond, Howard L. "Effect of Atmospheric Gas Supersaturation on Salmon and Steelhead Trout of the Snake and Columbia Rivers." *Marine Fisheries Review* 38, no. 7 (July 1976): 1–14.

Everest, Fred H. "Anadromous Fish Habitat and Forest Management— Economic Considerations." In *Western Proceedings: Fifty-eighth Annual Conference of the Western Association of Fish and Wildlife Agencies,* pp. 153–71. San Diego, California, July 17–20, 1978.

Federal Water Pollution Control Administration. "Summary of Water Quality Control and Management, Willamette River Basin." Portland, Oregon, January 1967.

Fish, F. F., and Hanavan, Mitchell G. *A Report Upon the Grand Coulee Fish-*

Maintenance Project, 1939–1947. Washington, D.C.: U.S. Fish and Wildlife Service, Special Scientific Report, no. 55, November 1958.

Fishery Development Program of the Columbia River, 1957. U.S. Fish and Wildlife Service, Portland, Oregon, September 1957.

Foerster, R. E. *The Sockeye Salmon.* Research Bulletin 162. Ottawa: Fisheries Research Board of Canada, 1968.

Frank, Bernard, and Netboy, Anthony. *Water, Land, and People.* New York: Alfred A. Knopf, 1950.

Fulton, Leonard A. *Spawning Areas and Abundance of Chinook Salmon (Oncorhynchus tshawytscha) in the Columbia River Basin.* Special Scientific Report—Fisheries no. 571. Washington, D.C.: U.S. Bureau of Fisheries, 1968.

Gile, Albion. "Notes on Columbia River Salmon." *Oregon Historical Quarterly* 56, no. 2 (June 1955): 140–53.

Gleeson, George W. *The Return of a River: The Willamette River, Oregon.* Water Resources Research Institute. Corvallis: Oregon State University Press, 1972.

Haas, James B. "Compensation for Salmon and Steelhead Losses on the Columbia River System." In *Columbia River Salmon and Steelhead,* edited by Ernest Schwiebert, pp. 176–79. Washington, D.C.: American Fisheries Society, 1977.

Harvey, Athelstan George. *Douglas of the Fir.* Cambridge, Mass.: Harvard University Press, 1947.

Hester, Frank J., and Sorensen, Philip E. *A Comparative Analysis of Alternatives for Limiting Access to Ocean Recreational Salmon Fishing.* Portland, Oreg.: Pacific Marine Fisheries Commission, April 1978.

Holbrook Stewart H. *The Columbia.* New York: Rinehart and Co., 1956.

Holland, G. A., Lasater, J. E., Neumann, E. D., and Eldridge, W. E. *Toxic Effects of Organic and Inorganic Pollutants on Young Salmon and Trout.* Research Bulletin no. 5. Olympia: Washington Department of Fisheries, September 1960.

Informal Committee on Chinook and Coho. *Reports by U.S. and Canada on the Status, Ocean Migrations and Exploitation of Northeast Pacific Stocks of Chinook and Coho Salmon, to 1964.* Portland, Oreg.: Pacific Marine Fisheries Commission, August 1969.

Johansen, Dorothy O., and Gates, Charles M. *Empire of the Columbia: A History of the Pacific Northwest.* New York: Harper and Row, 1957.

Johnson, Olga Weydemeyer. *Flathead and Kootenay.* Glendale, Calif.: Arthur H. Clark Co., 1969.

The Journals of Lewis and Clark. Edited by Bernard DeVoto. Boston: Houghton Mifflin Co., 1953.

Laythe, Leo L. "The Fishery Development Program in the Lower Columbia River." *Transactions of the American Fisheries Society* 78 (1948): 42–55.

Lorz, Harold W., Williams, Ronald H., and Fustish, Charles A. *Effects of Several Metals on Smolting of Coho Salmon.* Corvallis, Oreg.: U.S. Environmental Protection Agency, September 1978.

McKeown, Martha Ferguson. *The Trail Led North: Mont Hawthorne's Story.* New York: Macmillan, 1948. Portland, Oreg.: Binfords and Mort, 1960.

Morgan, Arthur E. *Dams and Other Disasters: A Century of the Army Corps of Engineers in Civil Works.* Boston: Porter Sargent, 1971.

Morgan, Murray. *The Columbia: Powerhouse of the West.* Seattle: Superior Publishing Co., 1949.

Morwood, William. *Traveler in a Vanished Landscape: The Life and Times of David Douglas.* New York: Clarkson N. Potter, 1973.

National Marine Fisheries Service, Northwest Fisheries Center. *The Snake River Salmon and Steelhead Crisis.* Seattle, Washington, 1975.

Neave, Ferris. "Ocean Migrations of Pacific Salmon." *Journal of the Fisheries Research Board of Canada* 21, no. 5 (September 1964): 1227–44.

Needham, Paul R. "Dams Threaten West Coast Fisheries Industry." *Oregon Business Review* 6, no. 6 (June 1947): 1, 3–6.

Netboy, Anthony. *Salmon of the Pacific Northwest.* Portland, Oreg.: Binfords and Mort, 1958.

———. *The Salmon: Their Fight for Survival.* Boston: Houghton Mifflin Co., 1974.

———. *Salmon: The World's Most Harassed Fish.* London: Andre Deutsh, 1980.

Oregon Department of Fish and Wildlife. *Maximizing the Return of Salmon and Steelhead to Oregon Fisheries.* A Report to the 1977 Oregon Legislature. January 1977.

———. *Willamette Basin Fish Management Report.* March 1, 1979.

Oregon Fish and Game Protector. *First and Second Annual Reports.* Salem, Oregon, 1894.

Oregon Fish Commission. *Biennial Report, 1953.*

Oregon State Board of Fish Commissioners. *First and Second Annual Reports.* Salem, Oregon, 1891.

Pacific Northwest River Basins Commission. *Anadromous Fish and Multipurpose Water Use.* Vancouver, Washington, 1979.

Pacific Packers Report, 1978. Camden, Maine: National Fisherman, 1979.

Parker, Robert R., and Kirkness, Walter. *King Salmon and the Ocean Troll Fishery of Southeastern Alaska.* Research Report no. 1. Juneau: Alaska Department of Fisheries, 1956.

Pettit, Stephen W. "Compensation and What It Means to Idaho." In *Columbia River Salmon and Steelhead,* edited by Ernest Schwiebert, pp. 169–72. Washington, D.C.: American Fisheries Society, 1977.

Porter, Russell G. *A Review of Limited Entry Alternatives for Commercial Salmon Fisheries.* Portland, Oreg.: Pacific Marine Fisheries Commission, June 1978.

Pruter, A. T. "Commercial Fisheries of the Columbia River and Adjacent Ocean Waters." In U.S. Bureau of Commercial Fisheries, *Fishery Industrial Research* 3 (1966): 17-68.

Raymond, Howard L. "Effect of John Day Reservoir on the Migration Rate of Juvenile Chinook Salmon in the Columbia River." *Transactions of the American Fisheries Society* 98, no. 3 (July 1969): 513–14.

———. "Migration Rates of Yearling Chinook Salmon in Relation to Flows and Impoundments in the Columbia and Snake Rivers." *Transactions of the American Fisheries Society* 97, no. 4 (October 1968): 356–59.

Rich, Willis H. *The Present State of the Columbia River Salmon Resources.* Oregon Fish Commission, Contribution no. 3. Salem, 1941.

Robinson, William L. "The Columbia: A River under Siege" (in two parts). *Oregon Wildlife* (Oregon Department of Fish and Wildlife), June 1978, pp. 3–7; July 1978, pp. 3–8.

Roosevelt, Theodore. *An Autobiography.* New York: Scribner, 1923.

Ross, Alexander. *Adventures of the First Settlers on the Oregon or Columbia River.* Edited by Milo Milton Quaife. London: Smith, 1849. New York: Citadel Press, 1969.

Royce, William F., Smith, Lynwood, and Hartt, Alan C. *Models of Oceanic Migrations of Pacific Salmon and Comments on Guidance Mechanisms.* Fishery Bulletin 63(3). Washington, D.C.: U.S. Fish and Wildlife Service, 1968.

Ruby, Robert H., and Brown, John A. *The Chinook Indians.* Norman: University of Oklahoma Press, 1976.

Scholz, Allan T., Horrall, Ross M., Cooper, Jon C., and Hasler, Arthur D. "Imprinting to Chemical Cues: The Basis for Home Stream Selection in Salmon." *Science* 192 (June 18, 1976): 1247–49.

Schultz, Leonard P. "The Breeding Habits of Salmon and Trout." In *Earth and Life,* vol. 2 of *Smithsonian Treasury of Science,* edited by Webster P. True. New York: Simon and Schuster, 1960.

Shepherd, Jack. *The Forest Killers: The Destruction of the American Wilderness.* New York: Weybright and Talley, 1975.

Silliman, Ralph. *Fluctuations in Abundance of Columbia River Chinook Salmon, 1939–1945.* Washington, D.C.: U.S. Fish and Wildlife Service, Fishery Bulletin 514, 1950.

Somerton, David, and Murray, Craig. *Field Guide to the Fish of Puget Sound and the Northwest Coast.* Seattle: University of Washington Press, 1976.

Springer, Vera. *Power and the Pacific Northwest: A History of the Bonneville Power Administration.* Portland, Oreg.: Bonneville Power Administration, 1976.

Sumner, F. H. "Age and Growth of Steelhead Trout, *Salmo gairdnerii* Richardson, Caught by Sport and Commercial Fishermen in Tillamook County, Oregon." *Transactions of the American Fisheries Society* 75 (1945): 77–83.

Townsend, John K. *Narrative of a Journey Across the Rocky Mountains to the Columbia River.* In Reuben Gold Thwaites, *Early Western Travels, 1748–1846,* vol. 21 (Cleveland: Arthur H. Clark Co., 1905). Also published by Ye Galleon Press, Fairfield, Washington, 1970.

U.S. Army Corps of Engineers, North Pacific Division. *Annual Fish Passage Report, Columbia River Projects.* Portland, Oregon, 1979.

————. *Water Resources Development in Oregon.* Portland, Oregon, 1977.

U.S. Congress, House. Subcommittee of the Committee on Appropriations. *Hearings.* 83d Cong., 1st sess., part 1.

U.S. Forest Service, Region 6. *Statewide Comprehensive Plan for Fish and Wildlife in the National Forests in the State of Washington.* Portland, Oregon, November 1978.

Van Hyning, Jack M. "Factors Affecting the Abundance of Fall Chinook Salmon in the Columbia River." Oregon Fish Commission. *Research Reports* 4, no. 1 (March 1973): 3–87.

Wahle, Roy J., Kaski, Reino O., and Smith, Robert Z. "Contribution of

1960–63 Broods Hatchery-Reared Sockeye Salmon to the Columbia River Commercial Fishery." National Marine Fisheries Service. *Fishery Bulletin* 77, no. 1 (1979).

Wahle, Roy J., and Vreeland, Robert R. "Bioeconomic Contribution of Columbia River Hatchery Fall Chinook Salmon, 1961 Through 1964 Broods, to the Pacific Salmon Fisheries." *Fishery Bulletin* 76, no. 1 (January 1978): 179–208.

Wahle, Roy J., Vreeland, Robert R., and Lander, Robert H. "Bioeconomic Contribution of Columbia River Hatchery Coho Salmon, 1965 and 1966 Broods, to the Pacific Salmon Fisheries." *Fishery Bulletin* 72, no. 1 (January 1974): 139–69.

Washington Department of Ecology. *Columbia River Instream Resource Protection Program.* Olympia, 1979.

Wendler, Henry O. "Regulation of Commercial Fishing Gear and Seasons on the Columbia River from 1859 to 1963." Washington Department of Fisheries. *Fisheries Research Papers* 2, no. 4 (December 1966): 19–31.

Wilkes, Charles. *Life in Oregon Country Before the Emigration.* Edited by Richard E. Moore. Ashland: Oregon Book Society, 1974.

Index

174 *Index*